Wealth Building Strategies of the Super Rich:
How to start a Family Dynasty

(Abridged Version)

Lionel "Luciano Illuminati" White

SPOIO Publishing (-_-),
an imprint of SPOIO Inc.
Virginia Beach, Va USA

www.SPOIOPublishing.com
www.SPOIOInc.com
www.LucianoIlluminati.com

Printed in the United States of America

ISBN 10: 1463768850
ISBN 13: 9781463768850

This publication is designed to provide accurate and authoritative information in regard to the subject matter covered. It is sold with the understanding that the publisher is not engaged in rendering legal, accounting, or other professional service. If legal advice or other expert assistance is required, the services of a competent professional person should be sought.

The cover photo is of a 1934 U.S. $100,000 dollar bill used by the Federal Reserve Banks.

Table of Contents

Chpt. 1 Introduction....................................5
Chpt. 2 Your Plan for Success....................11
Chpt. 3 Your Life Philosophy....................16
Chpt. 4 You've Got to Be Free....................24
Chpt. 5 Other Important Attributes.............32
Chpt. 6 Rich People Vs. Poor People.........40
Chpt. 7 The 9 Greatest Strategies...............52
Chpt. 8 Implement the Strategies...............54
Chpt. 9 Financial Education......................68
Chpt. 10 Start Your Family Dynasty...........94
Chpt. 11 Keep it in the Family..................107
Chpt. 12 Resources..................................113
Chpt. 13 About the Author.......................115
        Appendix.....................................118
        A: Jobs & Income Survey.............119
        B: Super Rich People....................127
        C: Most Profitable Industries........131
        D: Most Profitable Companies.....139
        E: Assets and Liabilities..............148
        F: More Great Quotes..................151

Chapter 1: <u>Introduction</u>

Many people are interested in the secret to wealth and riches. The phrase "the secret" is used to sell millions of books with various methods described that are supposed to give you an instant windfall. This book is not like those books for one simple reason: it contains the specific strategies used by the rich to build wealth. Just like everyone is different from every other person on earth in at least one unique way, there is no one way to obtain wealth that is right for every person to follow. There is a secret to wealth building however, but not just one method. Read on to discover what I mean.

When you look out upon nature with all it's beauty and wonder, one thing most people don't see is the viciousness of the survival cycle. Nice cuddly sweet animals are eaten by ferocious deadly ones. It is the way of the natural world. Natural selection chooses the most dominant individuals to survive and prosper and the others die off. There is no equality or fairness in nature. Human beings are not completely ruled by this anymore, but this natural world is still exerting an influence upon us.

Nature teaches us that the desire to survive is the strongest in the world. No creature on the earth wants to die. Every living thing is striving to have it's own space in the world and fighting to stay alive at the face of danger and uncertainty. No one is promised a next meal or shelter without hard work to obtain these things.

You must always remember that the nature of life is survival and to stay alive you must always keep the desire to survive. It is the same as your desire to succeed.

But success in life is a relative thing. Some people feel they are successful when they became a major league baseball player after many years spent in the minor leagues. Some people are successful when they get married to that special person who makes their heart swell with love and pride. You may feel that you want to possess hundreds of millions of dollars before you tell anyone that you have succeeded. The way you define success is really up to you. When you have it, it will make you happy inside in a way that nothing else will. But how do you become successful?

Can you get what you want in life or is it out of your control? How you answer that question will have a lot to do with whether you can or not. The great automobile manufacturer, assembly line innovator and one-time richest man in the world, Henry Ford once said: "Whether you think you can or whether you think you can't. You're always right." Believing in your own ability to accomplish great things is the number one trait of wealth building people. Believing in a predetermined destiny that has been set-up for you to stumble through life in darkness is not one.

Just think, if you miss out on your one and only chance to do something great then what will you do with the rest of your life? Sit around wallowing in your own misery? Blame that time that thing didn't work out for you? The choice is yours to make your own destiny, if you'd only believe it.

The main thing you need to remember is this: life is what you make it. You can not control every single thing that happens to you just by thinking about it, but you can control how you react to what happens. If you hold a positive outlook, then the problem is a chance to prove how smart you are at solving problems. If you hold a negative outlook, then the problem that shows up on your doorstep is a very bad house guest that ruins your day, night and weekend. You can't get any sleep, it won't leave and you can't get rid of it. Do you see the difference? Positive / Negative. Which one do you think you'll need to succeed? Which one is the greatest stumbling block?

Yes, many books have been written on the subject of money and wealth. This book hopes to be your road map to success by giving you not only the inspiration to achieve your dreams, but also the strategies to get you there. Like the saying goes: If you don't have a plan, then you plan to fail. I'd also like to add: If you don't know the road you need to take, then how will you get to your destination? Driving yourself through the perilous maze of right turns and lefts turns, u-turns and dead ends; you had better know the best road to take to avoid the potholes and gridlock along the way.

Most writers of this subject tell you the stories of great men and women who achieved great riches. They tell you what they did in particular to get those riches. This book will not tell you what to do in particular because I do not know what is going to work for you. What you need to learn is that rich people use certain strategies that middle class and poor people do not. That is the real secret to wealthy and luxurious living. Plus, you need to have your own ideas and your own visions.

Authors such as Robert Kiyosaki who penned Rich Dad Poor Dad says that the lack of financial literacy is the reason that his well-educated "Poor Dad" was penniless after years of dedicated hard work, so you can not become wealthy unless you quit your job and work for yourself. I disagree with this totalist attitude. You can make it any way you want to. You can work for a company, work for yourself or be a full-time investor. Any of these paths can lead to great wealth and self-sufficiency.

Do not let anyone tell you that you must follow their way or it won't happen for you. This author believes that anyone who uses the right techniques can accomplish great things regardless of the life story they have to tell. Reading this book will not require you to become a follower of me either. I will show you how to choose your own incredible yet true story of wealth accomplishment. If you want to follow a traditional course of working for a reputable co. because of the security and benefits then do so, just add the right strategy to increase your net worth. You can be a professor who gets rich or an entrepreneur who becomes wealthy, it's all up to you. There is no one path to success.

If you are looking for an idol philosophy to follow, you will be disappointed by this book. If you're looking to find your own way, then you will find it. You will need to know the best strategies of the super rich to get you there and that is exactly what this book will teach you. Do what someone else did if it suits you, but simply idolizing and copying someone great will not get you what they have.

Just Say No to Robert Kiyosaki's advice, his book should not be used to inspire the kids or teach them financial information. There are at least 9 powerful ways to become a more financially stable person that should be taught to every 16 year old before they leave high school. The problems of overspending and credit card debt getting out of control is a serious problem in our society today. If kids had this information they would be infinitely more equipped to deal with the world that is about to become very real to them. A story about a Rich Guy who dropped out of school at 13 is definitely not the kind of motivation that our kids need. At age 13, is there anything you can sell besides drugs?

I would like to reiterate that there is no one way to obtain wealth. If you want to be a more intelligent person then you use your natural abilities to learn. You put those abilities together with the best study techniques and you get smarter and smarter. The same goes for physical ability, the same goes for wealth.

You could get rich quick or it could take you half your life. You could marry a rich person or receive a huge inheritance from a distant relative you never knew. You could invent something that changes the world and you become an overnight success. There is no one way to achieve success just like there is no one way to define it. Everyone's life is as varied as the millions and millions of living things on this earth.

You know that deep down in your heart that anyone who tries to promise you or give you a guarantee that they can show you the foolproof way to get rich quick is full of crap. You know it, and I know it even though sometimes we fall for the scam because it's easy. But you also know that life is not always easy. Often times it's very hard, but no matter what it throws at you and no matter how hard it may seem to be at times; you control your outlook.

When you conclude reading this book you should have a

new perspective on how to accomplish your goals, a
strategic plan for doing it and a new understanding of the
best ways to accomplish them. You will know how to think
for yourself and make your own choices. The chapter on
Resources will help you to make those decisions and you
will become a more enlightened person on the subject of
wealth building and financial planning.

You can have all the abundance of the universe poured
down upon you like summer rain. With the right plan for
success, the right life philosophy, and the right strategies of
the super rich; you are on your way. You may have to
readjust your plans a little bit. You may need to scrap them
altogether and go with the most profitable move over the
dreams that could only take you but so far. It may be a
struggle to see yourself in a positive light because you've
never had it shown on you before. All these things may be
on your plate, but with the right wealth building strategies
and perseverance you will become wealthy and you will
start a family dynasty.

Chapter 2:   <u>Your Plan for Success</u>

The most important thing to do in starting a business up is writing a business plan. You almost can't get going without one. First you draft your mission statement. Then you write your strategic statement and finally you need the execution of the strategy statement. This is the same type of formula that you can use to make your "business plan" for your life. Or you could call it your plan for success. (SEE Appendix A: Jobs & Income Survey and Appendix B: Super Rich People)

What do you want to accomplish? That is your mission statement. You could say something like: I want to be rich, but that will not work for a good plan because it is too vague. All of the exact details must be included. A better mission statement would be: I want to possess 1 million dollars in 5 years. This statement is specific, but you could make it even better by saying: I want to possess assets worth 750 thousand dollars and 250 thousand dollars in cash money in 5 years. This statement is the most detailed and the most likely to work.

Next you need to write your strategic statement. This is the general explanation of what you need to do to accomplish your mission. You will need to research the tasks required to get the job done in the allotted time period. This is what businesses do to keep people motivated to reach their quarterly projections. You could say something like: I will get a job doing _____ making a $_____ a year salary and I will invest _____ dollars every year and make _____ dollars in interest or dividends from that investment.

Final Step: First I will apply for a position at _____
making $_____ dollars a year salary. I will contact
_____ to set-up an investment account. I will order a
financial research newsletter from _____. I will invest
$_____ dollars every year into a _____ account. I will
spend $_____ dollars every year on my household
expenses and personal needs. I will put $_____ dollars in
a savings account every year and in __ years I will have
_____.

		My Plan for Success	August 4th, 2009
	O		
		My Mission Statement:	
		My Strategic Statement:	
	O		
		Execution of the Strategy:	
	O		

Following a set list of tasks to achieve your ultimate goal is the best way to reach your dreams. Envisioning yourself having what it is that you want will help as well. Some people believe that if you paste pictures of the things you want on a poster board and hang it on your bedroom wall it will help you to obtain them. You look at the wish board everyday to keep your conscious and super-conscious mind working towards getting those things depicted from the images. Whether you choose to add this to your success plan or not is up to you, but it has been effective for some.

After you have your plan all done, make sure to date it so that you can keep track of how long you have to accomplish the goal. Put it in a safe place and then pull it out at least once a week to read it and mark off your progress. Or if you like you can post it where you can see it. I suggest you put a copy on your bedroom mirror if you have one or on the wall at eye level.

I like to put copies of my plans on all the four walls in my bedroom so I can always see it no matter what direction I'm looking. You should read it when you awaken and before you go to bed to fill your super-conscience (less positively referred to as sub-conscience) mind with the task at hand. But do not be fooled into thinking that all you have to do is think about it and it will all happen without your effort. That is a fantasy. You absolutely have to put forth a consorted effort with perseverance and fortitude.

Sometimes you won't accomplish your goal at first, but you will get closer and closer to it at every try. If you don't concentrate on it hard enough you may have to modify your plan and start over again. The idea is not to give up. Perseverance and fortitude is the key to success in any endeavor.

The more you think about something that you desire in life and put forth the necessary effort to obtain it, the greater the mental energy you direct towards it's materialization.

The secret to productive goal setting is in establishing clearly defined goals, writing them down and then focusing on them several times a day with words, pictures and emotions as if we've already achieved them.

--- Denis Waitley

This is the basic idea behind what is sold to people as The Law of Attraction. The concentration of mental energy focused on a specific thing or goal brings forth that thing or goal. But of course you need to do all the things that I have detailed in this publication to actually understand how the Law of Attraction really works. Follow the system layed out for you in this book and you will have anything you want in life, but you must remember that everyone's life and situation is different. You may take longer to grasp the concept then someone else and someone else may have been born on the top of the hillside with silver spoons.

You must remember always that there is no equality in nature. Some people will always have more than you and some will always be poorer than you as well. That is the Law of Polarity that states that there is no hot without cold, no up without down and no rich without poor. Cute animals get killed and eaten by vicious ones which maintains the balance of the habitat. And even though the smaller animals know that they are the hunted, they still strive to stay alive. No animal commits suicide in the wild, they push forward even in the face of extreme danger.

There is NO self-sacrifice for the King of the jungle and there can be NO self-sacrifice for you if you want to be the King or Queen of all your dreams. You must fight like the hunted and stand strong like the mighty lion. You can't give-up on life or your goals. Follow your plan for success.

Chapter 3: <u>Your Life Philosophy</u>

The ancient Egyptians believed that if you toiled your whole life away in poverty, giving away any extra money you came by and suffered, you would be rewarded with a workless existence where everything is handed to you on a silver platter in the after your life "other world." In other words you don't get the reward until after death. So they built huge shrines to house their dead pharaohs and the pharaohs ordered their servants to be killed and entombed with them after their death so that they would have their service in the after their life as well.

They also did not leave inheritances because all their stuff needed to be buried with them to be able to have it in their after their life. Thus the next generation always had it just as tough as the preceding one. The trinity of Father (Osiris), Son (Horus) and Holy Mother (Isis) held the fate of all mankind in their hands.

If you were a good person, when you died your heart was placed on one side of a scale against a feather on the other side and it was measured as being lighter than the feather because of good deeds. Then you were granted new life in the other world forever. If you were a bad person in life, then your heart would be measured as heavier than a feather and then you were punished by having a jackal eat your heart and your mummy which resulted in you remaining dead forever.

This belief served the pharaohs well since it kept the populace docile and obedient. They slaved away building temples and pyramids to fulfill the outsized egos of their kings and never strove for wealth. If the serfs ever protested because of the great toil and poverty that they had to endure then they were reminded of the future rewards after death. It was their life philosophy of a workless other world that made suffering acceptable to the peasants and slaves. The priests of this faith made a comfortable living off of preaching it to the masses while producing no evidence of it's validity. Nice scam, right?

Another Utopian dream that has been sold to people is that if you give up the right to ownership of your house, land and property and let the government own all the most important businesses then everyone will be equal. Everyone will get the same treatment and poverty will disappear forever. The thing about this scam is that when you eliminate the motivation of self-interest; people become slugs.

The government employees don't get a pay check based on the equality creed, they are the new masters because now they control the majority of people in the country who can not choose any other way to get their basic needs. They have no choice but to accept what is offered. Whom do they complain to? The government? The government controls the life and death needs of every person in the land and all the resources. Even better scam, right?

Equality of position for all people in society is a common theme of many communist doctrines, but it is all complete nonsense. You can not guarantee the desire of one man/woman will be equal to the desire of another. If I want it more than you, then I will most likely get it before you. The only way all the people will have the same things is to force the superior persons to downgrade to the mid-level or poor person. That is not a fair system because it destroys the human spirit and it is a definite violation of the basic individual human rights to be free. Many millions of people were killed and robbed during Bolshevik revolutions just because they were perceived as being rich or upper-middleclass. It is a sickness of the mind to think that you are helping society by forcing everyone to become equal by firing squad and piracy. If you want to be lazy and another person wants to work diligently then that is each person's basic human right.

There is no way to completely eliminate the differences in status, even when you have a whole new societal system; but you can choose to be better. Only the right strategies can make your life the way you want it to be. A theocratic monarchy or a dictatorship is a hard society to advance in, but in a free society; you can have it in life. The one and only life you're ever going to get. Don't get fooled again! Follow what "they" do and you'll stay on the bottom, but follow what the rich do and you'll come out closer to the top.

As a result of your efforts; you reap what you sow. Just as a cherry tree produces cherries and a grapevine produces grapes. A good farmer harvests what he/she has planted in an earlier season in a later season. A well-informed person makes decisions that are statistically superior to the un-informed person's decisions. There is an old saying that goes: It's not what you know, it's who you know. But in most cases, that is not correct. Who you know can help you, but what you know or what you think you know is definitely the bigger factor.

And your life philosophy is the most important factor of all.

It is how you see the world and yourself inside it. If you believe that you were created to serve a purpose that you can never really know then you harm yourself at every turn. If you believe that you are the master of your own destiny then you keep your options open and stay free to pursue whatever it is that you may be able to do to give yourself enjoyment and accomplishment. Whatever you want in life should be yours as long as it does not harm or infringe upon the rights to freedom of someone else. You are not born evil or fallen from grace. You are born free and you are born impressionable.

That is why if you were told that you were *inter urinas et faeces nasimur* - born between urine and feces or born between piss and sh*t (between the urethra and the anus is the vagina which leads to the birth canal) then you would probably have a very negative outlook on life. Even though there is nothing negative about natural birth, the way you say it makes all the difference. If you were told that a wife is a man's property, must be obedient to him and never deny him sex, cooking & cleaning and silence; then you will probably not believe that you have the right to have the same respect as men.

Woman are just as capable as men in many capacities. Of course there are certain things such as physical tasks where the majority of women are not as proficient as the average man, but that is not unnatural. Even in the inequality between men and women there is equality in mental ability, so women should not think that they are the inferior sex. But if you are indoctrinated from birth to believe that you are a subordinate or a servant then how can you see the truth of self-prophecy?

Differences of gender are natural, child birth through the birth canal is natural; but flawed dogma can crush a flower before it even has a chance to grow tall. Just as plants need good soil, water and sunlight to grow. The chlorophyll that makes them green also makes their food from the sunlight, the minerals in the soil and the water. It all adds up to just the right combination. Delete part of the equation or add some foul ingredient in and it dies.

That is why your life philosophy is so very important to your ability to have success. If you can't see it coming true then you are holding yourself back. And don't blame your parents for your failures either. They may have caused you to believe a stupid thing when you were little, but now that you're an adult it's totally up to you. What you think about yourself is what you let yourself become. You're a work in progress, no person is cast in stone at birth. Your mold is being shaped at every turn. You've got to be sculptor of your own manifest destiny and the architect of your own edifice of life.

Do you have a say in what happens to you or is it controlled by something? Are you the victim of fate or do you make your own way in life? Answer these questions the right way and it could equal a life of greatness. But answer them the wrong way and you will wallow in the mire. Mud and dirt will be your reward for a job well done of telling yourself that you can't instead of telling yourself that you can. The number one person that you will hear saying things to you, is you. So tell yourself that you have the strength to keep going. Tell yourself that it is not going to stop you. Tell yourself that everything is going to turn out right. You will get everything your heart desires.

It may sound funny, but some people have been trained to accept negativity in so much of their communication that it feels more natural than positive. Have you ever heard someone say any of the following: I'm no good at _____. I'll never get _____. I'm too _____ to be accepted. I'm too busy to _____. I'm too scared to _____. I can't _____. I'm not smart enough to _____. I can't afford _____. I'm too young to _____. I'm too old to _____. I don't have any help to _____. I will have too much family drama if I try to _____. I always fail at _____. How can this person ever overcome if they won't have faith in their self? No one else will believe in you if you can't believe in you either. To Be or not to Be, that may have been the question in William Shakespeare's Hamlet, but to be great or to be average is a question of life philosophy.

If you were scarred as a child and now you can't get the thought that you are stupid or sinful or too short or too poor or too plain or too ethnic out of your mind, please seek therapy if you need it. It can be a very tough thing to get over early childhood programing. Remember that many young children are taught to believe in a jolly old saint who brings presents to small children 6 days before the end of the year for being good and brings a lump of coal to them for being bad. This story is based on a real person, Saint Nickolas of Myra who was legendary in Europe, that did give to the needy in his area; but he wasn't able to fly a sleigh all over the world led by a reindeer with a bio-luminescent red nose.

Kids are told this lie, but they believe it because they don't know any better. Little children are put in a rather weird predicament by being born innocent. They can't decipher between a crazy fairytale and a scientifically proven fact, because they are naturally prone to trust their parents as authority figures. Almost anything will be believed by a child when it comes from parents, grandparents or teachers at a very early stage of their development. So you have to kill the demons inside with the grown-up of your inner child. Don't let the fairytales of yourself dictate who you get to be. It may sound like the truth, but if it has not gone through the scientific method of proof then leave it alone.

Your story won't be final until it's final; or as it is colloqially stated: It's not over 'til the fat lady sings. Re-write your script if it won't allow you to become a better person then some one else thought you'd be. Give your life expectency a revision of vision if it needs a new plot twist to make the hero get the girl/guy and run the villain out of town. The good guy always wins in the movies and you can win too. But not if you can't see it through, and not if someone else's negative story of you is still playing in your head. Or if your own self-limiting feature presentation is stopping your progress.

It has been said many times before, and will probably be said after now many more times. William Shakespeare's other well-known quote from Hamlet states:

This above all: to thine own self be true

Be true to your own greatness. Have faith in the unseen things that you will accomplish in the future. Plan your future and you will predict it better than any tarot card reader or i-ching practitioner. My life philosophy states that: **I can accomplish anything that I really set my mind to and work diligently to achieve.** You need a really great life philosophy too. Take the time to formulate one.

It will take you to the outer regions of the universe that formed so many billions of years ago and back. You will see the most minute of particles that were never seen with the naked eye and thought to be evil spirits causing disease for millions of years before humanity evolved and discovered the real hidden mystery of microbes; and even more.

A new world order is always coming on. A whole new world is happening right before your eyes every second of every day. Life is still happening as long as you're alive, so live it to the fullest while there is life to be lived. Your philosophy of life is the most important factor of all to achieving your success. So make sure you follow a brave creed that will give you all the inspiration you need to be all that you can be and more.

Chapter 4: <u>You've Got to Be Free</u>

This book is called Wealth Building Strategies of the Super Rich and I'm pretty sure you are expecting to be told a series of things that you can do to get rich and build wealth. That is ultimately the purpose of this publication, but first we have to make sure you are ready to put these strategies into practice. You've got to be free. The Beatles said that in Come Together. But what do I mean? You've got to be free. Well, you've got to be free to try different ways and means. You've got to be free to accept different theories that might not be the commonly accepted approach. You've got to be free to follow your own path.

Freedom is a word commonly used by people who are not free. They want to be free from oppression. They are oppressed because they can't vote, they can't love who they want, they can't believe the way they want, they can't divorce a spousal abuser without being shunned and some of the times they can't do anything they want because someone else owns them like a beast of burden.

If you do have freedom then you are not bound to someone's service, you can believe what you want, you can love whom you want and you can vote for what you want. That is what every oppressed person wants. Your belief system is just like this analogy. You are either oppressed by it or you are free because of it. If you are free then you make your own luck, no need to believe in lucky numbers, socks, or days. No need to be oppressed by lucky streaks and losing streaks that are beyond your control. You are not oppressed by elusive four-leaf clovers that grant good tidings and withhold them at their own discernment.

Life is exactly the way you think that it can be. If your parents were very poor and they told you that you'd be poor your whole life then you probably think that you'll be poor your whole life. It's not really the way it has to be, but it's your early programing. If you got good grades, had lots of friends, never got in trouble and got accepted into college with no need to pay your own way, then you'd have a pretty good outlook on your future. It's not a guarantee, but it's a product of *your* early programing.

Everybody got some sort of programing as a child. It could be helping you right now or hurting you. Sometimes people in our lives did damage to us unintentionally because that is the way they were taught as a child too. It is your job to determine whether your early programing is predominately positive or predominately negative. If it is encouraging or discouraging? Is it elitist or defeatist? You may think that is a strange question because elitist is usually looked at as negative, but that is because you were taught that forced equality is a good thing. But you don't need to do anything to keep people lesser or greater than you.

Remember the Law of Polarity? If there is hot, there must be cold, if there is light, there is also dark and if there is rich then there must be poor. And I know you're saying to yourself: "What about middle class? Your theory is wrong." Well, actually the law does provide for the middle ground as well. Yes, protons, neutrons and electrons have to exist, but you know that the middle class are just as susceptible to instant poverty as the poor. One bad thing like a job loss or a serious medical condition can change day into night. It's going to continue to happen whether you like it or not. There is nothing you can do about it but try to stay on the right side of the spectrum.

That is why I say that being elitist is not a bad thing. If you understand just how hard it is to pull yourself up out of the gutter, then you would not want your kids to get pulled back down into it. You would never want your children to have a harder life than you did. If you see this from the other side where the grass is greener, then you'd probably see it as just a protection mechanism. So therefore elitism should be defined as: The desire to associate with highly-rated people and that which is superior. It does not mean that you employ actions to keep certain people down.

You can't hold a man down without staying down with him.

--- Booker T. Washington

Remember, you don't control what other people's desires are. Your inaction or action can not make everyone rich or poor. But if you do try to keep other people down, then you should become aware of the Law of Karma - what you do unto others will be done unto you. You will be repaid for your actions with an equal and swift reaction. What comes around goes around.

Most rich people know what it takes to stay rich and one of those things is to not make the same choices as non-rich people. Your hard and smart work will be rewarded if you follow the right strategies. Rich people follow certain strategies and middle class people follow certain strategies and of course poor people usually follow certain ways too.

It is your challenge to figure out what the best ways are and how to implement them into your life. You want to be on the right side of the spectrum or you wouldn't be reading this book. You might not want to accept what is said here about the other side of the spectrum, but I know you don't want to test it out personally. No sane person wants to be poor. Have you ever thought about that? Only kooks want to be penniless and have to beg for their meals and receive give aways for their wardrobe.

No one but a fool wants to be a poor person. Being poor means you don't always have enough to eat. Sometimes it means you don't have a place to call your home. It could mean that your clothing is worn-out or very cheap and tacky. You are sometimes looked at as unintelligent just because your pockets are empty. Many poor people do not have access to good medical care and their health suffers because of it. It is not unheard of for poor people to die from common diseases that most people would receive treatment for and survive. Such is the life of many poorer people. You don't want this life.

You don't want the middle class life of living pay check to pay check either. A 30 year mortgage that can not be missed 3 times in a row without it going into default and then you loose everything you have put into it. You no longer have a home or technically you no longer have a house to call your own. Even though it was never yours to begin with. The company that owns it is letting you pay them for it over a long time period, but it's not like buying something from a store. When you pay for it, it's yours; you own the deed to it instantly. Not so with a mortgage.

Middle class should be a place you visit on your way to a city called Wealthy. If you are like most people, you want a decent income and a decent place to live. You want yourself and your children to receive good health care and to dress in clothing that is decent as well. You may not have it all, but you do have something. That is not a bad life, but there is much more if you ask for it. Just like the poem entitled <u>My Wage</u> by Jesse Rittenhouse that goes:

> I bargained with Life for a penny,
> And Life would pay no more,
> However I begged at evening
> When I counted my scanty store;
>
> For Life is a just employer,
> He gives you what you ask,
> But once you have set the wages,
> Why, you must bear the task.
>
> I worked for a menial's hire,
> Only to learn, dismayed,
> That any wage I had asked of Life,
> Life would have paid.

So is the message getting through to you now? Your life is what you make of it. Make it all that you want it to be or it will be whatever randomly happens to you. Don't ask life for the best and you will probably not receive it. So when I say: You've got to be free. Understand it like a cactus understands that it must keep the water that it absorbs during a rare rainfall for a non rainy day. Understand it like a worker bee understands that to protect the hive it must sting anything that disturbs it and afterwards it will surely die.

Understand that freedom of mind is the opposite of the

catholic church's oppression of the Renaissance's great astrologer Copernicus. He theorized that the earth was not the center of the solar system, but was in fact just a satellite of the all-mighty SUN. Nonsense the Vatican said. "The mind of a man can not know things that have not been explained thousands of years ago in stories compiled by celibate eunics hundreds of years after they were first written."

And of course the free person's mind *was* superior to the staid, dogmatic person's illogical mind. Freedom, I can't speak on it enough. I can't say enough about the power of free thought and exploration into the most magnificent under discovered region on earth: The Human Mind. Don't let your mind become trapped in a cell of old outdated traditions and rituals. Don't let it be taken over by hardline unbendable thought pirates. The booty is too valuable to lose, the loot is too illustrious to dispossess.

You've got to be free to become wealthy. Wealth is what people steal for, wealth is what people rob for and wealth is what people kill for, but you don't have to do anything evil to obtain it. Regardless of what you've heard, the love of money is not the root of all evil. The love of evil is the root of ALL evil. Don't believe it? Ask a serial killer if he was seeking a large pay day when he brutally murdered 13 people with a serrated knife. I'm sure you know he didn't do it because he loved money. Child rape is a moneyless evil as well. So get over the programming. It's not helping your situation.

Money is a conduit between you and what you desire to possess. You want it, she wants it, he wants it too. Once you have it, you want to keep it. Once you get it, you better protect it. Knowledge of right-minded thoughts is the power of the mind fully realized. The freedom to challenge conventional wisdom is the power to make your own energy. The light bulb above your head is gleaming and beaming a thousand points of candlelight power.

Do you need more inspiration? These words of wisdom are from great minds that have known the true meaning of you've got to be free. Read what some others have had to say about this subject.

Everything can be taken from a man but one thing; the last of the human freedoms - to choose one's attitude in any given set of circumstances, to choose one's own way.

-- Viktor Frankl

In the truest sense, freedom cannot be bestowed; it must be achieved.

-- Franklin D. Roosevelt

Freedom has its life in the hearts, the actions, the spirit of men and so it must be daily earned and refreshed - else like a flower cut from its life-giving roots, it will wither and die.

--- Dwight D. Eisenhower

Freedom is always and exclusively freedom for the one
who thinks differently.

--- Rosa Luxemburg

Freedom is not merely the opportunity to do as one
pleases; neither is it merely the opportunity to choose
between set alternatives. Freedom is, first of all, the chance
to formulate the available choices, to argue over them --
and then, the opportunity to choose.

--- C. Wright Mills

Chapter 5:   <u>Other Important Attributes</u>

You have learned that it requires many attributes to reach success. You have to formulate a clearly detailed plan, you need to have a positive life philosophy, and you've got to be free to think about different ways that may be unconventional to achieve your dreams. You also need to have perseverance to see the mission through to the end and you need the power to overcome adversity. All the knowledge in the world is of no use if your will is not strong and you can not keep the faith in yourself to vanquish the fire-breathing dragons that will try to block your path to success.

You will have to kill many demons along the way and you mustn't be too scared to scale the mountains that will try to hinder you on your journey to the other side where the streets are paved in gold and every garment is made of fine linen. To live the life is what you desire and it takes fire and determination. You can not be deterred by your own shortcomings, you must push on.

The successful man will profit from his mistakes and try again in a different way.

--- Dale Carnegie

Many of life's failures are men who did not realize how close they were to success when they gave up.

--- Thomas Edison

Every challenge is an opportunity to prove to the world that you are an Alpha Male or Female. You are the epitome of the great warrior of the past transformed into the high net worth hero of today. If things get hard, you get harder. You let the heat forge your core into a new alloy much stronger than nature ever intended. You stand defiant against the whirlwinds and all the storms that will try to blow you off course. The real secret to success is to never give up and never let anything or anyone outside of yourself stop you from reaching your dreams.

Microsoft Corporation was started on the 15th of September 1975 by Bill Gates, current richest person in the world 2009 and Paul Allen when they created the first version of MICROSOFT BASIC software for the MITS Altair; the first personal computer. In this same year, New York City ran into budget shortfalls and became severely over-extended. Their financial crisis got so bad that President Ford had to sign the NYC Seasonal Financing Act, which released $2.3 billion in loans to the city.

The government continued to issue loan guarantees and direct loans to support the fiscally-troubled city until 1986. All the loans, and fees have been repaid since that time and of course New York City has been fine since then. Microsoft's Windows operating system has allowed it to become one of the most successful companies in history despite being started the same year as a huge financial crisis.

The Allstate Corporation was started in April 1931 by insurance broker Carl L. Odell. He proposed the idea to Sears, Roebuck and Co. president and CEO Robert E. Wood. The idea for the company was to sell auto insurance by direct mail through the Sears catalog. Odell suggested that selling insurance by mail order could greatly reduce the costs by eliminating commissions paid to salesmen.

The idea appealed to Mr. Wood, and he passed the proposal on to the Sears board of directors, whose members were also intrigued by the concept and the Allstate company was born.

You are probably very aware of what happened in 1929; the Stock Market crashed and then during the first 10 months of 1930, 744 US banks failed (All in all, 9,000 banks failed during the 1930s) and it set off the Great Depression that lasted until 1940 when the US entered WWII. Allstate went on to become the 2nd largest insurance co. in the U.S., despite being started during the Great Depression.

The great industrialist, and quite possibly the richest person who ever lived, John D. Rockefeller of Standard Oil said shortly after the crash of 1929 that:

> These are days when many are discouraged. In the 93 years of my life, depressions have come and gone. Prosperity has always returned and will again.
>
> --- John D. Rockefeller

That's the attitude of a winner, even when the whole world is saying: "Woe is me, the sky is falling." You have to be able to see the cloud with the silver lining hiding behind the dark storm clouds looking ominously right before your eyes. The ability to stand strong in the face of adversity is by far one of the most valuable traits necessary to find your golden goose that keeps laying golden nuggets of wealth.

Diamond, emerald and ruby showers will pour down upon the person with the iron will to follow his/her plan for success to fruition.

Plant the seeds in good soil, water them daily, make sure they get the proper sunlight and watch them grow. When the time is right, they will feed you well. Repeat the process and they will feed you for a lifetime. The rains won't always fall when you want them to and the bugs will try to eat your crops as well, but if you keep the resolve even when everyone else is saying that all is lost; you will reap the greatest harvest.

A pessimist sees the difficulty in every opportunity; an optimist sees the opportunity in every difficulty.

--- Winston Churchill

Every adversity, every failure, every heartache carries with it the seed of an equal or greater benefit.

--- Napoleon Hill

All the knowledge that you have acquired through your conscience effort and your brain's non conscience efforts will assist you. They call this "common sense", and you should never ignore the voice in your head telling you that something is just not right or sounds a little out of tune or smells a little fishy. Allowing your common sense to guild you through the perilous journey of your life will give you a benefit that most people could have, but ignore. Conventional wisdom teaches that book knowledge is always greater, but I don't think so in all cases.

You must allow your super-conscience mind, that is always recording and indexing everything around you below your level of conscienceness, to speak out when something is out of sync with your plan for success and your life philosophy. This will save you and keep you from harm when you least expect it. So listen to your heart as well as your head in every endeavor. Keep your strong will and determination. The goals will become easier and easier with each successive accomplishment.

Oprah Winfrey is the mogul of Harpo Productions, actor, author, magazine publisher and talk show host of the Oprah Winfrey Show that airs in 140 countries. She is the first African-American woman to become a billionaire and she is worth about 3 billion at print time and growing. She started life in Kosciusko, Mississippi; being born to two very poor unmarried teenage parents. Her conception was due to a single sexual encounter between them, they broke up shorty after she was born. Her mother, Vernita Lee, was a housemaid, and her father, Vernon Winfrey was in the Armed Forces when she was born. He was also a coal miner, then he worked as a barber before becoming a city councilman.

After her birth, Oprah moved with her mother to live with her grandmother, Hattie Mae Lee, for the first six years of her life. She was so poor that she often wore dresses made of potato sacks, and the local children made fun of her. Her grandmother taught her to read before the age of three. At age six, she moved to an inner-city neighborhood in Milwaukee, Wisconsin with her mother. Her mother worked very long hours as a maid and didn't have much time for her so as a result was much less supportive and encouraging of her than her grandmother had been.

Oprah revealed to her viewers on a 1986 episode of her TV show about sexual abuse, that she was molested by her cousin, her uncle, and a family friend, starting when she was nine years old. After suffering many years of abuse, at 13 she decided to run away from home, but came back shortly. When she was 14, she became pregnant, but her son died a few weeks after birth. After this, her mother sent her to live with her father Vernon Winfrey in Nashville, Tennessee.

Vernon gave her a very strict home life, but he was very encouraging of her educational necessity. She became an honors student, was voted Most Popular Girl, joined her high school speech team at East Nashville High School, and placed second in the nation in dramatic interpretation. She won an oratory contest, which won her a full scholarship to the historically black college, Tennessee State University, where she studied communication.

At age 17 she won the Miss Black Tennessee beauty pageant and she also scored a job with the local black radio station, WVOL, which hired her to do the news part-time. She worked there during her senior year of high school, and also while in her first two years at TSU.

She became the youngest news anchor and the first black female news anchor at Nashville's WLAC-TV. She moved to Baltimore in 1976 to work at WJZ-TV where she co-anchored the six o'clock news. After then she was recruited to join Richard Sher as co-host of WJZ's local talk show: People Are Talking, which premiered on August 14, 1978.

She also hosted the local version of Dialing for Dollars there as well.

In 1983, Ms. Winfrey relocated to Chicago to host WLS-TV's low-rated half-hour morning talk-show: AM Chicago. The first episode aired on January 2nd, 1984. Within months after she took over the show it went from last place in the ratings to overtaking Donahue as the highest rated talk show in Chicago. It was subsequently renamed The Oprah Winfrey Show, it was expanded to a full hour, and was broadcast nationally beginning on September 8th, 1986.

She said on her 20th anniversary show that movie critic and former beau Roger Ebert was the one who convinced her to sign a syndication deal with King World. He predicted that she would generate 40 times as much revenue as his TV show, At the Movies. Her syndicated show quickly doubled it's national audience and displaced Donahue as the number one day-time talk show in America.

In 1993 Oprah hosted a rare prime-time interview with the late singer/entertainer Michael Jackson, which became the most watched interview ever and the fourth most watched event in American television history with an audience of one hundred million. In 1996 she started O magazine which usually features her picture only on every cover and Oprah's Book Club which has become one of the most influential in the world. Her endorsement almost guarantees the book will become a best-seller.She gives millions to charitable causes and she invested $40 million to start Oprah Winfrey Leadership Academy for Girls near Johannesburg, South Africa, which opened in January 2007.

This woman's life story is the epitome of overcoming adversity. She is the most influential and powerful woman on earth. If you can't achieve anything beyond mediocrity after reading this story then you need to close this book up right now and sit on your hands for the rest of your life.

Chapter 6:   <u>Rich People Vs. Poor People</u>

The times they are a' changin' Bob Dillon sings in one of his most popular songs. He was right, but the times don't change very much for those that have large amounts of money. They keep making more of it and poor people keep making less of it. Of course we live in a free society where anyone who works enough towards changing their situation can become more financially well-endowed. Anyone from the basement tenement can grow-up to build his skyscraper taller and broader than the world has ever seen. Few of us ever soars from rags to riches, but there is nothing stopping it.

You know what they mean when they say: this is the land of opportunity? They are telling you that we don't enforce a cast system; which is good for us, not so good for the 12th century adherents in other parts of the world. We understand that ancient people did not know everything, did they? They did know that building big strong (stone) structures that last for a very long time are better than weak (wood or aluminum) structures that are cheap to make, but fall easily. But they did not understand the full capabilities of the human brain to understand nature and themselves.

So what is it about rich people that makes them rich? Is it in the genes or can you get some of that too? Well, I will tell you from my research and observation; they have ways and means that are concentrated on making money. Rich people invest time and money on the science of making money and keeping money. They usually attend college to learn a trade that pays more than the average salary. They do not choose to labor physically at most of their jobs either. Let me explain further.

Rich people craft their plan for success from an early age with the intent to find a job that pays a larger sum of money than the average pay grade. While it is good to choose a career that you truly enjoy as in the saying:

Choose a job you love, and you will never have to work a day in your life.

--- Confucius

You should definitely look at a career choice from it's potential to enrich your life with a greater sense of capital. Love what you do *and* get paid more. Consider the advancement potential as well. It will give you fulfillment to be able to give to those you love and the less fortunate if you choose. Find a job you love so that it feels like you're not working. That is the message that Confucius was trying to convey. But I feel that it suggests that people do not want to have to work so they should choose the least unenjoyable job is the real message. To not have to work at all is the real goal.

Or you could say that people do not want to work very hard to maintain their lives. That is why so many pie-in-the-sky scams have been sold to people over the centuries. Do not let it happen to you. Learn what you have to do to get what it is you want out of life. No one can tell you what you should want and no one can guarantee that if you do exactly the same things as them then you'll get the same results. All anyone can ever do for someone else on a path of wealth discovery is provide some good advice and the financial education that is essential to success. If you have a desire

for it that burns hotter than the sun then you understand
what it takes.

Rich people understand that you need to put a certain
amount of money to the side for saving and another for
investing into income generating assets. The average person
lives their whole life seeking things that are wants only.
These are things that do not generate income and they
require the owner of them to pay more money to keep them
in proper operating condition. For example: an automobile
is an item that loses part of it's value right after you drive it
off of the lot. It requires repairs, replacement parts, oil
changes, new tires, and gasoline. Neglect any of these and
your car does not function properly anymore.

The automobile you own also requires licenses in some
states just to own it and one to drive it. More money, more
money, more money! Unless you use it for business
purposes such as delivery, it never pays you anything. And
this keeps happening for as long as you own it. The same
goes for a house that you live in. It may be your home and
your priciest asset, but it sucks the money right out of your
wallet/purse like a pickpocket in the airport. You never rid
yourself of this expense; but of course you need a house, so
you put up with things like a yearly tax bill to live in your
home.

I used a house and a car as examples because most people
are familiar with the expense of ownership of these two
items. Not everyone has owned a house or a car, but they
still have some knowledge of the situation to maintain
them. If you purchase a house that you do not live in and
you rent it out then it becomes an income generating asset.
It generates income for you and your family. You may say

to yourself: "We need to sell the house that we are moving out of."

There is the difference between you and a rich person. They understand that real estate ownership management is one of the best ways to make money. Not everyone can afford a house or their credit is not acceptable when just starting out, so they rent a nice house before they try to buy one.

Why not make some money off of this natural phenomenon to pay off your mortgage and then take in extra money? You could hire a service company to take care of it if you don't feel up to it. This little baby step into real estate could lead to buying more houses and making more money once you learn to walk. When your credit gets good enough you could purchase an apartment building and make even larger sums of money. Once again a service co. could handle the management of it.

You have to retrain your thinking to see opportunity at every turn. There are lots of ways to make more money without actually working another job. That is what poor people think is the best way to supplement their income. "Honey, we need more money. I've got to get another job." But why not take a small amount of money and invest it to have your money working for you. That is what every rich family does to make money without actually physically working. There is only a certain amount of time that can be spent physically working and all work and no play is a terrible way to live.

Poor people spend a large percentage of their extra money on trying to impress their friends and neighbors with the latest gadgets and the newest model of car. They call that:

Keeping up with the Jones. Rich people understand the value of things that accrue in value such as a fine painting, a classic car that can usually be purchased for only a few thousand dollars, fixed up and then resold for thousands more, and stocks, bonds and other securities.

These are the subjects you need to study to better yourself. If you do not feel comfortable with making your own stock picks then you could hire a broker, but there are computer programs that can do most of the decisions for you as well. They use formulas and algorithms to predict the best companies to invest in and the best time to buy and sell. You just follow it's lead and learn as you go along. Research newsletters are also available that are written by teams of financially proficient people who eat, live, and breathe financial information. You can learn this stuff.

Rich people have more leisure time and poor people have very little. The higher grossing jobs of the rich provide as much as one full month of paid vacation time and usually 2-3 weeks of paid personal time; not to mention 2-3 weeks of sick leave per year. Many poorer people do not receive any money for taking time off at all. Sick days usually equal a deficit and there are no personal days to claim.

When you dream you are asleep, but when you envision you are wide awake. So take your dreams and bring them into the real world. When you plan for success you are putting energy out into the universe that has to come back to you eventually. That is why your plan for success has to have complete details as to what you want. All the people who want to be rich that merely state an incomplete order to the universe wonder why all the techniques they heard about don't produce the same results for them. It's not because they are bunk, it's because they are not being specific enough to make it work.

I told you before to craft your plan for success. You may want to revise it now that you understand the differences between rich people and poor people more clearly. You should be able to see, feel and hear this message much better than you could when you first starting reading this book. Every lesson learned is a new neuron growing connections in your brain.

Rich people Vs. Poor people is not a very fair fight. You know who the winner is and who is the loser in this competition. You know which one of these is usually the healthiest, you know which one of these usually has the most enjoyment in life. You are well aware of which one of these that you want to be. Therefore, do what it takes to be more successful. Learn the ways and means of making larger sums of money. Choose a career you can love that pays more, love is *not* all you need. You need much, much more.

It is said that poor people pay interest and rich people make interest. They make money off of their money. They take a small percentage of their income and turn it into more money. Poor people usually have a fear of any kind of investment besides the state lottery. They lose a substantial amount of money from paying credit card interest, late fees and overdraft charges to their banks. Grow-up if you want to play with the big boys and girls. The land of the rich and invested is not the playground of toddlers. Force yourself to balance your budget, pay on time and don't use the credit cards if you can't pay more than the minimum balance. Pay them down and then keep them for a rainy day.

Rich people are predominately business owners, investors, entertainers, inheritance recipients, CEOs, content owners (copyright, trademark, patent), doctors, lawyers, dentists, statesman, commercial bankers, computer software engineers, professional sports competitors and high ranking managers. They are not very commonly lottery winners, organized crime criminals and people who just find bags of money laying on the ground right in front of their path. You have to choose to be rich and hopefully you won't choose a criminal path, because it usually ends in prison or death.

You did not choose to not be born rich, so you definitely have to make a concentrated effort to become a wealthy person. You can use your talent, your knowledge or your creativity, but you have to work smart. If you don't like to make decisions then the decisions will be made for you. The universe is abundant and generous. There is more available then any of us could ever use in twelve lifetimes. We share this earth with millions of known living things and many more unknown ones. We alone have the capacity to think about our place in the world and alter it to suit our desires.

Want more with every fiber of your being and never give-up easily. If you have exhausted every possible option to the fruition of your vision then it *is* time to give-up, for a moment. Just take a little time to recharge your battery and start again with a new and better vision. Never truly give-up. Self-made rich people did not give-up on their plan to become rich. They don't believe that it has to be accomplished from one way only and then if that doesn't work then give-up. They just keep trying different ways to get the wealth they crave.

Rich people use their creativity to make themselves money and poor people use their creativity to make other people money. Almost everyone has to toil for someone else when they first start working, but there comes a day when you have to seize it.

Carpe Diem – Seize the Day!

--- Horace

Find the courage to be your own boss. Business Owner is the number one highest money making title of the rich and CEO is the number one highest money making position (anesthesiologists earn a higher average, but requires huge insurance coverage). If you do not have the creativity to come up with a new business, then buy one or buy stock in one. Look into securing a loan for a franchise. The bank will feel much more confident in your ability to repay the loan because of the support from the parent company and because they will be responsible for the majority of the advertising of the brand.

You just punch right into a successful business without all the fear that it might crash & burn quickly and you lose everything. This is a good option that should not be overlooked. The 100 richest people in the world all own stock in companies. Most of them started their own company or bought some. In the ancient world the richest people were rulers of countries that fought and defeated other kingdoms and then stole their fortunes, but in today's world the corporate kingdoms are tops.

Poor people don't see all the opportunity circling around them because they are too concentrated on survival and material items. They dream of the lavish lifestyle of the rich and famous because it is the outward display of the life that they want. You will get to surpass all The Joneses in your life if you can learn to postpone your need for immediate gratification.

When a person attends a university they are not considered to be a scholar after the first or second year. They have to keep at it until they pass all the tests to be awarded a certificate of completion. You have to do the same thing when pursuing wealth. You have to keep pushing towards that goal, until you have passed all the tests to be awarded a better life for yourself and your children.

Our goals for wealth building should include others as well. There is probably no greater feeling than to know that your loved ones will be taken care of in the unfortunate event that you don't live forever. We all hope we do not have to die, but if you leave the world as a wealthy person then your loved ones should be alright financially.

Poor people don't usually leave their loved ones with anything but sadness, tears and bills when they die. You don't want to be a burden in death, make sure they have fond memories of you and your money --- you won't need it anymore. Whatever motivation you have, please keep it. Rich people leave money, stocks, bonds, annuities, houses, businesses, jewelry, paintings, trust funds and life insurance payments to their loved ones.

The next generation has a good headstart because of their good educations and the good size inheritances left to them. Don't you want your kids to have a better start than you did? Don't you want them to feel confident about their future?

Wealth building is starting off with a good education (whether self-taught or school taught), deciding on a good career path based on proper knowledge of income potential (SEE Appendix A: Jobs & Income Survey), drafting a good plan for success, implementing that plan and then reaping the benefits. Once you reach one goal then strive for another one. Put a percentage of your money in savings, invest a certain amount in stocks and bonds, or other income generating assets and plan for your retirement.

You may have to cut back on luxuries right now to have even more in the future, but it is well worth it. Don't eat out at restaurants so much. Make your own lunch; it is probably better food anyway. Disconnect the cable/satellite tv until you can afford it. Share one car, carpool or take the bus or subway until you start making more. Forget about the most expensive designer brands until it no longer causes you to have to consider what you must go without to obtain them. Don't be afraid to be thrifty and save money by using coupons and special deals. A dollar saved *is* a dollar made :)

There are a few more things to learn about before the strategies are revealed. Rich people don't kick their children out of their homes at 18. They allow them to finish college and purchase a house of their own before they decide to leave. Sometimes they pay for college and buy a house for them nearby. Some children of the rich even marry someone first; and perhaps stay in a guesthouse on the property or in their original room for a few years before moving out. Poor people can't wait to force their kids out into the street with no money, no permanent place to live and student loans to pay.

Rich People Vs. Poor People will continue on forever, but if you know how to navigate the treacherous waters filled with sharks and killer squids ready to devour you at every turn then you will become wealthy. Talented actors, writers, musicians and producers make money from what they write, produce and perform and receive royalties into perpetuity, but most people have to plan wisely for a residual income. Most people have to plan wisely to receive multiple streams of income. Most people don't have any plan to receive more than one income at all.

Rich People Vs. Poor People can be summed up as the dichotomy between master and servant. There are basically two types of mentalities, the master mentality and the servant mentality. When you are in charge, the boss, the owner, the lord (as in landlord, lord of the manor, etc.) and possessor of a master's degree; then you are the master. And when you are the subordinate, the employee, the workerbee, the sharecropper, the proletariat; then you are the servant. It is not an insult, but the reality of existence. Most people are workerbees and only a few people are royals or Queen Bees. Work as hard as you may with the servant mentality but you will never become the queen of the hive.

Changing your mentality is the only way to become more than what you are right now. You may never truly live a life of fulfillment if you don't. If you want a beautiful life that is much more than the average then you must change it. Servants die and are only remembered by their friends and relatives, but masters live forever through their accomplishments and achieve true immortality.

Your descendants will stare at a portrait of you on the wall in the great room of your palatial estate and wonder how did you get so great? What an incredible blessing it was to be born into your family. The knowledge that you pass down to them will enrich and bless them with all the wisdom and understanding of how to build wealth and to keep it. They will be so proud of you and you will never regret becoming their hero or heroine.

Chapter 7: The 9 Greatest Strategies for Building Wealth

Each of the following strategies can be used singularly or in combination to get you the richer life that you seek. Put them into practice and you will become wealthy today, not someday.

(Listed in order from the most greatest to least greatest)

1) Start and run a business (preferably with limited liability), buy and run a business (preferably with limited liability) or buy stocks/bonds or other securities in a corporation or government

2) Buy real estate to develop the land, sell the property and the land or rent out the property

3) Work in the entertainment industry as a performer (actor, musician, singer, dancer etc.) and ascend to stardom, or work as a manager, agent, producer or director

4) Work as a professional sports competitor, manager, agent, coach, sportscaster or announcer

5) Create or buy intellectual property such as: trademarks, patents, copyrights; songs, literature, screenplays, music, designs, photographs, films, tv shows, slogans, jingles, art and software

6) Study very hard and get a college degree that will allow you to have a high-paying career (doctor, dentist, lawyer, professor, statesman, etc.); save and invest your

money wisely

7) Become famous (fame makes your presence, your image, your life story and your opinion much more valuable than a non famous person or group; the same goes for property and a brand)

8) Accept free money; prizes, inheritances, trust funds, grants, gifts and marriage to a wealthy person or a person from a wealthy family

9) Play games of chance: gambling, state lottery

Like I said at the beginning of this journey, everyone is a little different than everyone else, but we are all the same in our desire for wealth. To reach our goals it requires a plan for success, a free mind, determination, the ability to overcome adversity, and the right strategies to choose from to make the goal a reality. Take what you have learned here and make it come true. Use the advice in the next chapter to implement the strategy(ies) that best fits your idea of what you want in life. Then use the instructions in Start your Family Dynasty to continue the trend and give your kids a good headstart.

Chapter 8:   <u>Implement the Strategies</u>

Now that the greatest strategies have been revealed to you, choose your path wisely. Nothing comes from nothing so be prepared to give something if you want something to be given to you. Research what you need to do to reach the goals that you have chosen. Intelligent concentration is absolutely required to get from point A to point B, from entry to extraordinary, and from launching pad to stratosphere. Have no fear and carry your shield of forged knowledge and wisdom. It will protect you from the weapons of all your adversaries and guarantee: You will be Victorious.

If you choose to start a business then you must be knowledgeable of the industry, the costs and legalities of setting it up and the equipment needed to run the business. You should have an original name that is short and easy to pronounce like SPOIO (spy-o). Look it up on the net to see if it is in use and conduct a trademark search. Check with your state to see if the name is available for legal registration as soon as possible. These things will save you the frustration of choosing a previously registered name. It is also a good idea to check the availability of a good URL to be used with it. Websites are a very necessary business tool in today's world. Most people expect you to have one.

There will be many other things to consider such as if your idea is too common to be a likely success. This is a very hard decision because it can make you feel like a failure before you even get started, but it will save you a lot of frustration. You are not a failure just because your first idea needs to be revised. Revise it if necessary and then research your new idea. (SEE Appendix: Most Profitable Companies, Most Profitable Industries) When you have satisfactorily prepared yourself to be your own boss then do it. There is no right time to do it, just do it. Only fear will advise you to postpone for no good reason. If you have the money, the time and the inclination then you are ready.

If your choice is to join another group of business owners in a franchise organization then you should research the best franchises on the web or find an industry association that can give you very up-to-date information. Find the company that's right for you and seek financing if needed. The company should have a training program that will teach you and your managerial staff the entire process of running the business. Once you have satisfied their requirements then you are a proud new business owner with a support system and parent co. advertising and probably a regional owner's ads program that will help with ad costs. If you want to buy an existing business, conduct extensive research.

Buying stocks and bonds can be a very daunting task. You will need to familiarize yourself with the stock market, brokerage houses, and brokers. You don't have to use a broker, but you must learn to read financial papers or purchase a computer program that can assist you in picking your securities. It can be very beneficial to take a class or attend a seminar. Most successful investors have a long term investment strategy, but you will make your choices based on your own situation (SEE Appendix C: Most Profitable Industries).You can hire a financial adviser to help you plan this out.

One type of program that is not widely promoted is buying stock directly from a company or their representative and not through the stock market. These programs are called: DRIPs. It stands for Dividend Re-Investment Plan. You can invest a certain amount of money and then set a certain percentage of your dividends to be reinvested every payout back into the portfolio. This gives you a higher stock ownership without putting in any more money. You can also choose to have a small amount of your capital gains paid out to you and let the remainder be reinvested.

If you choose a good category to invest in such as utilities or energy then you could make a very nice return with little effort. The reason I like these types of stocks is because everyone needs them, plus utilities are required to provide service by law. In other words: They can't go out of business.

If a utility company can't maintain it's geographic area then another company has to take it over so that those people and businesses will have electricity. Energy is a requirement in today's world. Gasoline, natural gas and electricity are solid. Emerging sources of producing energy such as wind and solar power are coming on stronger and in the future they could be responsible for 20%.

When choosing to buy stocks in known companies, it is a good idea to choose companies that have a steady history of paying dividends. Some very popular brands never pay any, so your only profit is from short selling the stock at a higher price than what you paid. Think about private companies, they are not subject to stock market fluctuations. Get someone you can trust to advise you.

Real estate is the ownership of land and property on land. Do you think this will cease from making money? Research this industry thoroughly before you jump in. Attend seminars, classes and read books on the subject. Look into the gov't programs to assist buyers. Check foreclosure listings in the newspaper, from banks and from the gov't seizure agencies. Good deals can be had from other people's inability to keep their mortgage going. Unfortunately this is the biggest purchase that most families make so it is the number one thing they lose as well when times are tough.

Adjustable rate mortgages are a big contributor to foreclosure. The low introductory rates convince gambling people to make a gamble that the rate won't increase too dramatically. It usually shots up in a few years to beyond their means or someone loses a job and can't pay. Developing land is another area of real estate that you could profit from. It helps if you are very knowledgeable of zoning laws, building codes and construction procedures.

Renting out your old house after you move into a new one can be a good way to get into property management. You don't have to manage it yourself if you don't feel like fixing toilets on Saturday, you can hire a service company to do this for you. Again, lots of research should be conducted to determine such things as; 1) is this area good for renting out? 2) can we afford to make a mortgage payment (if you still have a mortgage) and a tax payment if we don't have a tenant? And 3) will it make more money as a rental than selling it?

You will make the right decision with good advisers and good research. Different strategies should be explored such as renting a property out in a down market and not flipping it. Buying property exclusively for renting it out can be very lucrative if you get the right location (location, location). With enough money and credit you can buy an apartment building or commercial building and have a steady income along side your work income. Hugh fortunes are made doing this business.

I am pretty sure that you are aware that some of the richest people in the world are participates in the entertainment industry. If you are a popular musician who also writes songs then you can get paid millions from the performance, royalties from the record sales, the publishing royalties and the airplay or other usage of your songs; 4 different checks. Most performers do not make millions of dollars though, but if you are a star and you know it; then make the world see it too. Study your craft, practice it everyday, and don't give up. Don't listen to detractors if you have fans.

If you have NO fans then quit. If no one likes anything you do then you are probably not talented enough to make history. If you listen to more criticism than people listen or watch you, then you should save yourself the embarrassment. This industry is super tough. Only those with "IT" truly find the pot of gold at the end of the rainbow. Most entertainers struggle to make more than $50,000 a year, but some make as much as 40-50 million a year. According to Forbes Magazine, talk show host and production studio owner: Oprah Winfrey has made at least 225 million a year since 2005.

However, all the money is not made only by the guy/gal in the spotlight; the managers, directors, producers and agents make tons of money as well. Follow your dreams and reach for the stars. But don't be fooled like most people. Your talent will only take you half way there. You will have to present an original character, theme or personality to be able to breakthrough. Believe in yourself and make 'em believe in you 100%.

Only a very rare person is capable of playing for a professional sports league. Practice your assets off. No, not really. Assets should be kept unless you get a very good offer. Practice, study your hero's moves and make them your own. If you play a team sport, respect the team and heed these words:

> The way a team plays as a whole determines its success.
> You may have the greatest bunch of individual stars in
> the world, but if they don't play together,
> the club wont be worth a dime.
>
> --- Babe Ruth

Give your pursuit the passion and heart that is needed to be a champion. Use your head more than your competition by studying what they do as well as what you do. Always know them better than they know themselves. Visionalize yourself making all the right moves before a competition and you will become the multi-millionaire pro sports star that you seek to be. Keep your image clean and you will make even more money from endorsements then you receive from the sport.

Tiger Woods, the great African/Asian American golfer, has been rated as the highest-paid athlete by Forbes Magazine since 2005 when he made 87 million dollars from tournament winnings and endorsements. As of Oct. 2009 he has made a total of 1 Billion dollars. The Russian born tennis player, Maria Sharapova, made an estimated 18.2 million and was the highest-paid female athlete of 2005. She signed with talent agency IMG at age 11 and has made tons of money from endorsements.

Most sports competitors are out of the professional game after 10 years, but there are some where you can keep at it for a long time such as golf. In golf you first play as an amateur then in the Nationwide tour if not good enough for the major pro league which is the PGA tour or Lady's PGA called LPGA; and finally once you are older (usually 50) you can play in the Champion's tour if you are a champ. You could make very good money doing what you love past 50 or 60 years old. Auto racing also gives this type of opportunity, but not so in most sports so you need to prepare for early retirement.

Sports managers, agents, coaches and announcers have just as much staying power if not more than the players who usually retire after a decade or so because of injury. You can keep raking it in for a long time in these other positions. A former player can also extend his fame and million dollar salary with an auxiliary sports career. Do the math, read the play book, watch the game tapes --- there is a fortune to be made from the sport of playing games. If you have the skills, you can pay the bills.

Creativity is the source of infinite energy. The wellspring never has to run dry. The amount of money that can be made from creating intellectual property content is boundless. Buying this content and housing it to be licensed for usage is also a very profitable profession to engage in. Research the various ways devised to protect your work such as trademark, copyright and patent. Explore the different methods used to distribute your content such as radio, tv, satellite, syndication and the internet. Learn the industry you want to conquer and make it your conquest to utilize as you see fit.

Content is King and ownership and creation of content is a kingdom maker. Use what you've got to get what you want. Your intellectual property can be licensed to other countries and translated into different languages to ad infinitum. Most rights to making money off of it lasts for a very long time. You and your beneficiaries can receive royalties from a book for your lifetime plus 70 years.

The most common way to obtain wealth is to study hard and receive a college degree in a field that pays a large salary, save some money and invest some. You will need to research the income potential of various careers that interest you and then craft your plan (SEE Appendix: Jobs and Income Survey and Super Rich People). Follow it and start to live your dream. You can do it with the proper attitude that you've learned. Seek financial knowledge and then save and invest your money. Do not choose a mortgage that will get you into trouble. Live below your means as much as possible and one day you will become wealthy.

Use credit cards sparingly and for emergencies mostly. Or a good strategy to use is to pay for everyday things with one credit card and pay it off at the end of every month before the interest is added. This will build up a good credit record with little risk of surpassing 80% of your limit. Keep your limit at least 20% open so that your interest rate will remain low and pay on time every time.

Use the equity in your home to re-invest in more profitable

investments. For example; if you have $100,000 in home equity and you take it out and put it in a savings acct. with 8% annual interest then you'll have $215,887 after 10 years. You could use it to pay off your mortgage early or you could continue to pay on a mortgage and then use your home equity as your personal bank. You could also get a reverse mortgage, which is open to seniors of 62 years with atleast 40% home equity, it is a loan that does not need to be re-paid until 12 mths after you die or move out of the house. Contact HUD.

There is a good reason that moms want a doctor or lawyer in the family. These two career choices, along with dentist, provide for a very steady and lucrative lifestyle with both paying in the low six-figure rage. You really can't go wrong with a career that serves a constant need in society, but you will make your own decision based on what appeals to your personal interests and intellectual level. If you do choose one of these careers your family will benefit from the free consultations/diagnosis that you know you are obligated to give them, but you shouldn't mind helping them stay physically and financially healthy if you truly care. So study like crazy; you will need the best grades.

Contrary to some people's beliefs, you can work a steady job, use investment strategies and become a wealthy person. There is no need to forgo your dream job because you don't feel like it will pay you enough to have the type of life you want with a nice house and a large family. You can have it all. You will just need to plan it out more carefully with the help of trained individuals who can show you step by step how to put aside a certain amount of money that is good for you in particular to accumulate a sizable retirement fund or annuity and a for-income-now investment fund.

Some people will hate that this is listed as a top strategy, but it is a fact of life. Fame makes a person's opinion, presence, image, and life story much more valuable than a non famous person. You or your brand can sell much more of anything if made famous. Famous actors, professors, sports competitors, etc. make more than their counterparts. Fame is a boost to most professions. Famous doctors can guest on TV shows, famous teachers and politicians become personalities that are paid to speak at events. Famous CEOs write books and become even more successful :) The list goes on and on.

Your skies have no limit when you add fame to the equation; $Y + X$ = more money. It does not matter what Y is if X = fame, you will benefit from a greater sense of awareness. If more people know your brand, it will receive more customers, clients, members, or whatever. Get yourself some of this elusive gold dust and sprinkle it all over you. The gold rush will be epic like 1849.

Seek the services of PR firms, hire an agent or study up and do it yourself. Advertise, write articles, write books, make videos and post to the web, get interviewed: Get Famous. Receive more attention from the opposite sex that can lead to love, money and fandom. Fan loyalty can pay you more after your heyday is over than you made during your glory days. Just ask the Eagles and the Rolling Stones who rake in more from their touring than more current acts. Fame is a stimulus for all other strategies of wealth building; Get Some.

If you accept money that is freely given to you for no

reason whatsoever than because someone wants you to have it, it is a blessing. Let yourself become more financially endowed by simply receiving an inheritance or applying for a grant or marrying into a wealthy family. You may need to be nice to an elderly relative, but no one should have to pay their relatives to be nice to them. So be a dear, it pays. You may need to research who is giving away money through which foundation or gov't agency and apply for as many that apply to you. No real work involved when you consider the rewards of efforts put forth.

So get some of the free money that flows like the Colorado River from the rich up on top of the mountain down to the less rich down in the valley every single day. Small amounts of accumulated wealth always equal more wealth at the end of the day just like large amounts that accumulate all at once. Lump sums or annuities, it does not matter because money is money. One dollar collected from one hundred people is the same as one hundred dollar bill received from one person.

And as for marrying money; it has been done for centuries by royals. They marry someone else that is royal so that the kingdom expands or a treaty with a former enemy can be established. The blue bloods and celebrities do the same thing to keep the money flowing into the next generation. You have probably heard of the question: For Love or Money? That is for you to decide. Some people will call it gold-digging and some will see it as strategic life planning.

Especially when you want to be rich and you consider that 50% of divorces are because of money issues and a large percentage of spousal murders are because of life insurance, it makes sense to seek financial excess more than absence in a mate. Though traditional men who want to take care of a woman usually ignore her income level. If you are fortunate enough to find someone who loves you that is from a rich family then you should go for it because poverty will tear your relationship apart.

There is really no way to have an opinion of money that is given freely out of love. The person giving it is the source of the boost to your self-worth so be thankful. Of course there are things that you could do to target a potential mate that is wealthy or is from a wealthy family, but it may backfire on you. I believe that it is best to marry for love, but use your head before you make that final decision. Love is not all you need so check the financial history and the plans of your love interest. Their past may be shaky, but if they have a good plan for the future you should let love rule.

The least valuable strategy to build wealth is to play games of chance or to play the lottery. This method involves the most risk of complete lose of investment. That is why it is last on the list of greatest to least greatest. On a scale of 9 to 1, you have a greater chance with all the other strategies than this one. Use it with caution and don't go overboard. Do not gamble money that you need to use to pay important bills. **Only gamble what you can afford to lose.**

If you are a master of some particular game of chance then by all means: Get that Money! It can be very invigorating to win BIG in Las Vegas or Atlantic City. Some very gifted people gross millions of dollars in prize money each year from their gaming skills. But for most people this one should be used with extreme caution and extreme skill.

Lotteries are the daydreams and night dreams of most average middle class and poor people. However, most rich people are not recipients of state lotteries. The winners usually give too much away to friends and relatives and then overspend on luxuries. After a few years most of them are poor again. If you do win the big prize you should immediately consult a tax and finance adviser to invest your winnings and pay your taxes so you don't get charged with tax evasion.

After you live it up or travel a little bit, get back to real life. Research what you can invest in to maintain your winnings beyond the stereotypical lottery winner's short nouveau riche time period. Don't become a negative statistic. You can become a wealth builder just like those who work for it and have their money working for them and have others working for them if you use your mind. Enjoy the easy money, take it easy and be easy going. You didn't work for it, so give some to less fortunate people (you will feel much better), but don't get guilt robbed by your family and friends.

Wealth, however legally obtained is a blessing to it's owner and it's owner's family. You have done a very good job of Living the Dream. You have become a legend in your own time. You are not a failure, you are a winner. So act like it. Dress like it. Talk like it. Walk like it. Be the ideal that others look up to. Be the role model for success that you were inspired by as a child. The cycle of the charmed life is complete when you teach the next generation. So please teach the children well and they will lead the way to more greatness for themselves, you and your Family Dynasty.

_Dream lofty dreams, and as you dream, so shall you
become. Your vision is the promise of what you
shall one day be; your ideal is the prophecy
of what you shall at last unveil. The greatest
achievement was at first for a time a dream.
The oak sleeps in the acorn;
the bird waits in the egg.

--- James Allen, from As a Man Thinketh

Chapter 9: <u>Financial Education</u>

You may be feeling a little anxious to get going, but there is something that you should have that is the ultimate unifying principle: Financial Education. I should not assume that you are knowledgeable about the different types of investments and bank accounts and such so therefore this chapter will cover the basics about financial education. If you are an expert on the subject then please skip ahead to the next chapter. For everyone else this is very important information that can definitely help you to make better decisions when you attempt to implement the strategies that are best for you.

Most middle class and poor people are poor and middle class because of their lack of financial education. Most rich people are wealthy because of their financial education and utilizing their advisers' information. This is probably the one type of knowledge that should be taught in high school, but is usually not taught. If you want to be rich, you have to understand investments because investments are the most practical way to increase your net worth without working for the money. And if you want to stay rich you have to understand how to balance your budget, choose the best wealth building strategies for you and general financial information.

The first thing you need to do to get on the right track is to make a list of all your monthly income and your monthly expenses. This is called making a budget. A budget will help keep you from overspending on unnecessary things that will keep you from having that extra money to save and invest. It is very wise to not only invest for your retirement, but also save money for an emergency and use savings accounts and investments to build up your net worth.

Some people will tell you that savings accounts are the investments of scared people who are too afraid of risk, but that is nonsense because you can use compounded interest to give yourself a nice return with zero risk of losing the money. The account is protected up to $250,000 per depositor by the Federal Deposit Insurance Corporation (FDIC). The amount used to be $100,000 per depositor and $250,000 per married couple with a joint account, but it has been temporarily increased for an individual depositor until December 31, 2013.

It would be foolish to not use a safe investment option to balance your more riskier ones. Stocks and bonds are not insured by the FDIC. You could lose your entire investment or have it reduce in value and present a loss when you sell it off. Balance is a state of the universe that produces order out of chaos. We live in an ordered existence so keep balance in your actions to stay in sync with the flow of the world. You have probably heard financial advisers say: "Diversify your portfolio." Well, it is sound advice. Don't risk everything for the gamble of making a lot, because it is not guaranteed.

Let us get back to the first lesson at hand: Balancing Your Budget. Table 1 is an example of what your budget should look like. You can add more categories if you need to, this one is just general. Subtract the total of all your monthly expenses from your income and then use that extra money to save and invest. You could start a savings account and a retirement account such as an IRA if you don't have a company sponsored 401(K) plan.

[Table 1]	My Monthly Budget
Rent or mortgage payment	
Electricity payment	
Natural Gas payment	
Water payment	
Cable / Satellite Tv / Internet payment	
Phone payment	
Car loan payment	
Car insurance payment	
Health insurance payment	
Life (or Disability) insurance payment	
Renters or Home-owners insurance payment	
Groceries	
Medicine	
Restaurants / Eating out	
Entertainment	
Miscellaneous expenses	
XXXXXXXXXXXXXX	XXXXXXXXXXXXXXXXX
Extra Money to Save and Invest	

Now that you have balanced your budget, let's make sure that Rich Dad Poor Dad has not warped your brain with Robert Kiyosaki's false definition of the word asset. His most famous statement is that: "A house is not an asset." So what is it then? An asset is any property that has a commercial value; it can generally be sold and make a fair market amount of money for the owner. A liability is a debt; it is money that you owe such as a loan, credit card balance or a home mortgage. A house is an asset!!! A home *loan* is a liability. If this is false then the Federal Reserve is wrong too.

An income generating asset is what Robert tells his 26 million readers to find and utilize. Now that is good advice. The mistake that he makes is in telling you that because your home ownership involves additional expenses then that means it is not an asset at all. This makes *No* *s*ense and should be grounds for 26 million refunds given out to customers of his books. Every single thing that you own has the potential to cost you money to repair or fix it up after time, not just a house which gives you a tax deduction from interest paid on a home loan. What crap Robert Kiyosaki is mis-teaching people!

I guess this word-defining guru has never heard of renting out a room, attic or basement in your house, turning it into a duplex or renting out another property for money. You also produce income from a house you own that accrues in value and then you sell it. Nothing but narcissism tells a person that the accepted meaning of a professional word like asset is unacceptable to them and that everyone else should follow their definition of it instead. I think most psychiatrists would define him as an egomaniacal charlatan.

[Table 2]

Assets		Liabilities	
Cash		Home loan	
Savings/Check-ing account(s)		Home equity loan	
Money Market account(s)		Car loan balance(s)	
Certificate of Deposit (CD)		Credit card balance(s)	
Home Equity		Student loan(s)	
Real estate (land/property)		Business loan (s)	
Market value of car(s)		Child support (per year)	
Market value of boat(s)		Hospital and medical bills	
Stocks/Bonds / Options		Miscellaneous	
Mutual Fund (s) or Annuity			
401(K) retirement plan			
IRA/Roth IRA			
Art/Paintings/ Collectibles			
A Business or Businesses			
Intellectual property			
Miscellaneous			
Total Assets		Total Liabilities	

Subtract your assets from your liabilities and that is your net worth. Assets – Liabilities = Net Worth.

Once you have determined your net worth, you can devise ways to increase it. The best way to do that is to increase your income generating assets which are property that can increase in value or produce a return from interest or dividends. (SEE Appendix E: Assets and Liabilities of Households) Here is a list of the most common income generating assets:

Income Generating Assets

Savings account(s)
Interest-bearing checking account(s)
Money market account(s)
Certificate(s) of Deposit (CD)
Stocks / Stock Options
Bonds
Mutual fund(s) or Annuity
A room in your House (for rental)
Real estate (residential rental property)
Real estate (commercial rental property)
A Business or Businesses
Intellectual property (royalties - songs, patents, etc.)

Income generating assets are what separate the rich from the poor. Rich people work for money and make money work for them and poor people work for money only. And when you're poor or middle class, your main contribution to the economy is to support the income makers of the rich. They are producers and you are consumers. You are taught to have one source of income, and they are taught to have multiple streams of income. That is why poor people can't catch up to rich people by simply working only. Maybe you got a great throwing arm and you make the pro football team and get paid millions, but it's not the most common scenario; so learn how the super rich get wealthier or stay poor. The choice is yours. It is very easy to be mediocre, it is very challenging to soar with eagles.

Change your gameplan or nothing will change for you in your life. Still looking for the key? Still searching for the secret? All of this information is needed to increase your income, increase your net worth and become a wealthier person. Financial education is so pivotal that you could take a thousand get rich quick courses and stay pathetically penniless for the rest of your life. Study this info until you know it intimately, use it to your advantage and you will become wealthier.

Always remember that nature does not provide a perfect and fair life for you or any living thing on earth. Plants, trees, birds, mammals, reptiles, and microorganisms can all die from disease. Life is too short to waste your time. You will never get back all those years, and months and days and minutes and seconds you throw away. Your life is precious, treat it as such. If you want a better life, you better work for it. If you want to be rich, you better learn to think like a rich person.

Now that you have found the extra money to put some of your monthly income into a savings account, you should decide which type is good for you. There are a few different savings accounts to choose from. Here is a detailed description of each type:

Types of Savings Accounts

Savings account
• You can access your money at any time.
• You earn interest on your money.
• You can easily move your money from one account to another.
• Your savings are insured by the FDIC up to $250,000 until December 31, 2013. After then it reverts back to $100,000 per depositor & $250,000 per joint account for a married couple

Interest-bearing Checking account
• This is just like a savings account but you get checks or a checkcard (debit card) to use with it

Money market account
• You usually earn a higher rate of interest then a general savings account.
• You do not have to pay any fees if you maintain a certain minimum balance.
• You may have check-writing services.
• Your savings are insured by the FDIC up to $250,000.

Certificate of deposit (CD)
• You earn interest on your money during the term (three months, six months, a year or 2 etc.).
• You must leave the deposit in the account for the entire term to avoid an early withdrawal penalty.
• You receive the principal and interest at the end of the term.

• Your savings are insured by the FDIC up to $250,000

You can use the compound interest of a savings account to take a small amount of money and turn it into a larger amount of money. Interest is paid on the original deposit and the earned interest as well. Rich people use this to make money off of their money so that it seems like they never stop making more money even when they don't work. It can work for you too. This is probably the safest way to use your money to make more money.

Like I said before: Rich people earn interest and poor people pay interest. The compound interest of a credit card with a 22% interest rate is the reason why you can't pay off a $1,500 balance only making a minimum payment of $50 a month until 4 years has gone by and it will cost you $700. That is why so many people get trapped by an open line of credit such as a credit card. It can be damn near impossible to get out of this trap if you keep adding more purchases and only paying the minimum payment. Avoid this hazard and use the same compound interest to help you, not hurt you.

There are several different ways a savings account can be set up with compound interest. Here is a list to explain:

Daily Compound Interest – the annual rate is divided by the days in a year and then the daily rate is applied to each day's beginning balance. The formula for a 365 day method is:

$$\frac{\text{Annual Rate}}{365} = \text{Daily Rate}$$

Monthly Compound Interest – the annual rate is divided by months of the year and then the daily rate is applied to each month's beginning balance. The formula for a monthly method is:

$$\frac{\text{Annual Rate}}{12} = \text{Monthly Rate}$$

Quarterly Compound Interest – the annual rate is divided by 4 periods of the year and then the daily rate is applied to each quarter's beginning balance. The formula for a quarterly method is:

$$\frac{\text{Annual Rate}}{4} = \text{Quarterly Rate}$$

Semi-Annual Compound Interest – the annual rate is divided by 2 periods of the year and then the daily rate is applied to bi-annual beginning balance. The formula for a semi-annual method is:

$$\frac{\text{Annual Rate}}{2} = \text{Semi-Annual Rate}$$

Annual Compound Interest – the annual rate is applied to the balance once a year.

To use these formulas to figure out how much you would make if you deposit a certain amount each month, then just add the amount and multiply the rate as usual. For example, if you have an account that is compounded monthly at 6 % you would apply the monthly rate plus the monthly deposit and repeat the process 12 times.

First deposit of $1000 Annual Rate is 6/12 = .5% (mthly rate) Balance is $1005.00

1st mth interest earned = 5.00

Balance is $1005.00 + 125 (mthly deposit) x .5% (mthly rate) = $1135.65

2nd mth interest earned = 5.65

Balance is $1135.65 + 125 (mthly deposit) x .5% (mthly rate) = $1266.95

3rd mth interest earned = 6.30325

As I'm sure you can imagine, this progress will continue on until you have amassed a sizable fortune. If you continue to deposit $125 a month at 6% interest compounded monthly then you will have $125,000 in 30 years. If you have a $10,000 balance and you make a $1250 deposit a month compounded monthly then you'd have $50.00 in interest the first month before the deposit and then $56.50 interest earned for a total of $11,356.50 after the first month. Just imagine the pay off after 30 years on this formula. There are many charts and calculators that you can use for specific amounts and rates.

For example, If you are 20 years old and would like to have $1 million by the time you reach age 65 then the following chart will show you what you need to invest today at a 10 percent return, compounded annually. If you can invest $13,719 today, it will grow to $1 million over the next 45 years. You never have to add another dime to your initial investment. Whatever age you are, you can use this chart to figure out how much you need to invest to reach your financial goal.

Age	Amount invested	Amount invested	Amount invested	Amount invested	Amount invested
20	$2,743.00	$5,487.00	$8,232.00	$10,976.00	$13,719.00
25	4419	8838	13257	$17,676.00	22095
30	7117	14234	21351	28468	35585
35	11462	22924	34386	45847	57309
40	18460	36919	55378	73838	92296
45	29729	59458	89186	118915	148644
50	47879	95757	143635	191514	239392
55	77109	154217	231326	308435	385543
60	124185	248369	372553	496737	620921
65	200000	400000	600000	800000	1000000

This chart shows the results of a 10 percent return that is compounded annually.

In order for you to choose the best investment option, you need to know what each type has to offer, the risks involved and the benefits. Here is a detailed listing to help you make an educated decision:

Stocks - owning a part or share of a company. You are referred to as a shareholder, stakeholder or stockholder. You make money from your investment when you sell the stock to someone else for a higher amount then you paid for it. It has to increase in value to do this or you lose a part of your investment if you sell it at a lower cost which is called depreciation. You also make money from receiving a dividend which is a payment from the company's profits that is paid out quarterly, bi-annually or annually.

Options are contracts to buy or sell 100 shares of stock at a certain amount in the future. A *call* is the right to buy 100 shares before a specified expiration date and a *put* is the right to sell 100 shares before a specified expiration date and at a specified price which is called the *striking price*. You make money by selling the option when the current market value of the stock is higher then the striking price of a call or lower than the striking price of a put. You may exercise the option and buy/sell the stock, cancel the option before the expiration date and sell it off for profit or let it expire and lose your total investment. Detailed training is necessary to understand how to use this investment tactic effectively. It involves substantial risk, but a hedging strategy can be used to generate huge profits.

When you purchase stocks you are not protected by the FDIC, you could lose your money. You are taking the risk that the company could go out of business or it's stock could lose value. Before you decide to invest you should study financial projections for the co. and the industry using a broker, computer programs, newsletters or websites for independent investors. Look at the past performances and the management, the products and any other info you can get. Stock prices usually depreciate or appreciate based on reaching or not reaching quarterly projections. Make an informed decision and don't pick stocks for novelty reasons. (SEE Appendix: Most Profitable Industries and Companies.)

Bonds – lending your money to a company, federal, state or local municipality. A bond is like an IOU for corporations and the government. The issuer of the bond makes a promise to pay a certain rate of interest during the term of the bond and to repay the entire face value when it reaches maturity. The interest rate is mostly based on the credit rating of the issuer and the current interest rates. Moody's and Standard & Poor's are firms that rate bonds. For most corporate bonds, the company's bond rating is based on its financial health. For municipal bonds, the rating is based on the creditworthiness of the public or other governmental entity that issues it.

The issuers with the greatest likelihood of paying back the money in full and on time are given the highest ratings, and their bonds will pay an investor a lower interest rate. The issuers with a lower credit rating are less likely to pay it back in full and on time so their bonds have a higher interest rate. These are sometimes called junk bonds.

A bond can be sold at face value (referred to as *par*) or at a premium or a discounted price. An example of this would be when the prevailing interest rates are lower than the bond's stated rate, the selling price of the bond rises above its face value and it is sold at a premium. Contrarily, when the prevailing interest rates are higher than the bond's stated rate, the selling price of the bond is discounted below the face value. Bonds can be kept to maturity or traded.

Another type of account that could be useful for people with a low income is called an Individual Development Account. An IDA is a part of a money-management program organized by a local nonprofit organization and

generally opened at a local bank. The deposits made into an
IDA account are sometimes matched by deposits from a
foundation, government agency or other organization.

IDAs can be used to buy your first home, to pay for your
education, for job training, or for starting a small business.
Budgeting, saving and managing credit training programs
are often a part of IDA programs. To find out more about
IDAs call: CFED at (202) 408-9788, or visit its website at
www.idanetwork.org.

Savings bonds - a U.S. Savings bond is a government-
issued and government-backed loan to the government.
There are several different types of savings bonds with
slightly different features and advantages. The *Series 1*
bonds are indexed for inflation with an earnings rate that
combines a fixed rate of return with the annualized rate of
inflation. Savings bonds can be purchased in denominations
ranging from $50 to $10,000.

Treasury bonds, bills and notes - these are bonds issued
by the U.S. Treasury to pay for a variety of government
activities and are backed by the full faith and credit of the
federal government. *Treasury bonds* are securities with
terms of more than 10 years and the interest is paid semi-
annually. *Treasury bills* are short-term securities with
maturities of three months, six months or one year and they
are sold at a discounted price from their face value. The
difference between the cost of it and what you are paid at
the maturity of it is the amount of interest that you earn.

Treasury notes are interest-bearing securities with
maturities ranging from two to 10 years with the interest
payments made every six months. *Treasury Inflation*

Protected Securities (TIPS) is a security that keeps pace with inflation and the interest is paid on the inflation-adjusted principal. Treasury bonds, bills and notes are sold in increments of $1,000. These securities, along with U.S. savings bonds, can be purchased directly from the Treasury through TreasuryDirect at www.treasurydirect.gov.

Some government-issued bonds offer special tax advantages. There is no state or local municipal income tax on the interest earned from Treasury and Savings bonds. In most cases, the interest earned from municipal bonds is exempt from federal and state income tax. Many rich people invest in these bonds for their tax benefits. You can purchase stocks, bonds and mutual funds through a fullservice broker if you need investment advice, from a discount broker if you can decide on your own, or even directly from some companies and mutual funds. When investing in these products you should always remember to do the following:

• Find some good information to help you make informed decisions.
• Make sure you know and understand all the costs associated with buying, selling and managing your investments.
• Beware of investments that seem too good to be true; because they probably are.

Mutual funds are funds established to invest many people's money in many different firms. When you buy shares in a mutual fund, you become a shareholder of a fund that invests in many other companies. A mutual fund diversifies it's interests to spread risk across numerous companies rather than just relying on one company to perform well. Mutual funds have varying costs associated with owning them, such as management fees and fees for withdrawal. The degrees of risk will vary depending on the type of investments the fund makes. Before investing in a mutual fund you should learn about its past performance, the companies it invests in, how it is managed and the fees investors are charged. Learn what the professionals say about it and similar funds.

The Rule of 72

The rule of 72 is a very good tool you can use to help you estimate how your investment will grow over time. Simply divide the number 72 by your investment's expected rate of return to find out approximately how many years it will take for your investment to double in value. For example: if you invest $10,000 today at 8 percent interest then divide 72 by 8 and you get 9. Your investment will double every nine years. Your $10,000 investment will be worth about $20,000 in nine years, about $40,000 in 18 years and $80,000 in 27 years. Here is the formula:

$$\frac{72}{\text{Interest Rate}} = \text{Years to Double}$$

It is not an exact tool, but it can help you make a better judgment of your investment choices. There is another area of financial education that you should also understand, and that is income generating assets. Remember, this is the way to wealth accumulation if you do not receive a large salary. A large salary is most poor people's dream, but it's rare and not really necessary if you plan effectively. Starting or buying a business is another very good way to increase your income and net worth. The richest people in the world and throughout modern history have owned and started businesses. Here is a listing of business types with their advantages and disadvantages:

sole – proprietorship – a one person owned business that only requires the purchase of a local municipal business license to operate and registering with the state tax authority. This is the most popular business type with more than twice as many as any other. The advantages of this business entity is that it is cheap to start-up and cheap to run. The disadvantages of this type of business entity are numerous.

It is difficult to get a loan (capital) because the owner has to guarantee the loan with personal assets along with the business assets. You could lose anything that you use as collateral to back up a loan. A lawsuit against this type will be paid from the business and the owner. You have 100% liability for the debts of the business because the debts of the business are the responsibility of the owner. The business can not live on after the death of it's owner. Most rich people do not set-up this type of business, or they only use it to start out and then upgrade to a business entity with limited liability.

Partnership – two or more person owned business that only requires the purchase of a local municipal business license to operate and registering with the state tax authority. It is exactly the same as sole-proprietorship accept for the the shared ownership. Each partner contributes money, property, labor and/or skills, and agrees to share in the profits or losses of the business. The advantages are cheap start-up cost and operation. The disadvantages are that you have multiple people who have to agree on the management and operation and it has unlimited liability.

Just like the one person business it is difficult to get a loan (capital) because the owners have to guarantee the loan with their personal assets along with the business assets. The partners could lose anything that they use as collateral to back up a loan. A lawsuit against this type will be paid from the business and the owners proportionally to their ownership share. You have 100% liability for the debts of the business because the debts of the business are the responsibility of the owners. This type of business also ends with the death of one of the owners, you will nccd to find a new partner if it was only a two person partnership and file an application for a new partnership if any partner leaves.

Some rich people do set-up this type of business, it is popular in the construction business. But it is troublesome so they may only use it to start out and then upgrade to a business entity with limited liability. You can have many different arrangements with a partnership. Here are some details of the other types of partnerships:

Limited Partnerships - a limited partnership is a business partnership formed by two or more persons and having at least one general partner and one limited partner. General partners retain control over the management of the limited partnership and are liable for all the debts of the business. The limited partners invest money or property in the business and are entitled to share in the profits, but their liability is limited to the extent of their investment. You form this entity by filing a certificate of limited partnership with the State Corporation Commission and pay a filing fee.

<u>Limited Liability Partnerships</u> - both limited partnerships and general partnerships may register for status as a limited liability partnership by filing a statement of registration as a registered limited liability partnership with the State Corporation Commission paying the filing fee. Many lawyers, doctors, and dentists form this type of business because you can not sell stock in a medical or law practice on the stock market. The obvious advantage is limited liability for business debts.

<u>Limited Liability Company</u> - a limited liability company is an unincorporated business which provides owners with limited liability similar to the kind available to shareholders of a stock corporation. It may also be treated as a partnership for tax purposes. It can be owned by one or more people who own portions of it and are referred to as members. You need to file articles of organization with the State Corporation Commission and pay a small filing fee. You must acquire a license from your local municipality as well and register with the state tax authority.

The advantages of this entity is that it has limited liability which means the owners are not personally responsible for it's debts. It is easier to get capital than the other types listed. The disadvantages are that the ownership can not be sold on a stock exchange like a stock corporation. Each member must be happy with whom the membership shares are sold to.

<u>Business Trust</u> - business trusts are unincorporated businesses, trusts, or associations governed by a governing instrument that provides for the property or activities of the business trust to be owned, managed or carried on by at least one trustee for the benefit of at least one beneficial owner. The beneficial owners are usually entitled to the same limitation of personal liability as the shareholders of a stock corporation. You have to file articles of trust with the State Corporation Commission and a nominal filing fee. Trusts are very popular with the wealthy to keep the family money managed and distributed in a wise manner to future generations.

Corporation – this is the best type of business entity to set-up if you want to become a rich person. It can be formed by one or more people by filing articles of incorporation with the State Corporation Commission and paying a fee. You then need to purchase a municipal business license and register with the state tax authority. A corporation provides you with limited liability for the business debts proportionally to your personal equity in the company and it can exist perpetually.

You may purchase stock with money or by trading valuable property. Stocks can be bought and sold directly from the company, through fullservice brokers or through online discount brokers. It is much easier to raise capital because of the rather smooth process of selling shares. This is just one of the reasons that a corporation is a true money maker of the super rich. Create one today if you want the best tool of the wealthy at your disposal. A company needs to be managed by directors of the board who are usually shareholders, they vote on matters such as hiring the CEO (Chief Executive Officer) and very important decisions. It consists of 4 officers: president (CEO), vice-president, treasurer (CFO: Chief Financial Officer), and secretary.

Retirement Funds

401(k) Plans

Many companies offer a 401(k) plan for employees' retirement. Participants authorize a certain percentage of their before-tax salary to be deducted from their paycheck and put into a 401(k). Many times, 401(k) funds are professionally managed and employees have a choice of investments that vary in risk. Employees are responsible for learning about the investment choices offered. By putting a percentage of your salary into a 401(k), you reduce the amount of pay subject to federal and state income tax. Tax-deferred contributions and earnings are the best method to use in investing. In most cases, your employer will match a portion of every dollar you invest in the 401(k), up to a certain percentage or dollar amount. Which of course is free money or an addition to your income.

As long as the money remains in your 401(k), it's tax-deferred. Withdrawals for any purpose are taxable, and withdrawals before age 59½ are subject to a penalty. You should definitely take full advantage of your company retirement savings programs because they are great ways to build wealth.

Qualified Plans (formerly referred to as a Keogh plan) -

a qualified plan is a tax-deferred plan designed to help self-employed workers save for retirement. The most attractive feature of a qualified plan is the high maximum contribution—up to $42,000 annually. The contributions and investment earnings grow tax-free until they are withdrawn, when they are taxed as ordinary income. Withdrawals before age 59½ are subject to a penalty. Check the IRS web site—www.irs.gov—for current information on tax-deferred investments.

Individual Retirement Accounts (IRA)- an individual retirement account lets you build wealth and retirement security. The money you invest in an IRA grows tax-free until you retire and are ready to withdraw it. You can open an IRA at a bank, brokerage firm, mutual fund or insurance company. IRAs are subject to certain income limitations and other requirements. You can contribute up to $4,000 a year to a *traditional IRA*, as long as you earn $4,000 a year or more. A married couple with only one person working outside the home may contribute a combined total of $8,000 to an IRA and a *spousal IRA*.

Individuals 50 years of age or older may make an additional "catch-up" contribution of $1,000 a year, for a total annual contribution of $5,000. Money invested in an IRA is deductible from current-year taxes if you are not covered by a retirement plan where you work and your income is below a certain limit. You don't pay taxes on the money in a traditional IRA until it is withdrawn.

All withdrawals are taxable, and there usually are penalties on money withdrawn before age 59½. However, there are a few withdrawals you can make without penalty, such as to pay for higher education, to purchase your first home, to cover certain unreimbursed medical expenses or to pay medical insurance premiums if you are out of work.

A *Roth IRA* is funded by after-tax earnings; you do not deduct the money you pay in from your current income. But after age 59½ you can withdraw the principal and any interest or appreciated value tax-free.

Pension Fund – a retirement account set-up by a company or government that is unfunded or funded by investments to build up a large fund from which to pay retired persons a monthly stipend. Similar to a 401(k), but less portable and with very specific ages of benefit. Sounds good enough, except you can loose the ability to receive this money if you are fired before the required amount of years and then leave your job with a small to ZERO amount of retirement money until you qualify for Social Security. There are two types: 1) defined-benefit – employer guarantees a definite amount regardless of the fund's performance 2) defined-contribution – the amount received is determined by the amount contributed and the fund performance. Both types also use: amount of pay at retirement, age at retirement and years on the job as other criterion for the amount paid out to the pensioner.

The U.S. Office of Personnel Management runs the (FERS) Federal Employees Retirement System that consists of a 3-tiered plan: Social Security, Basic Benefit Plan; which you may withdraw if you leave federal employment, and thrift savings plan; which is like a 401(k) with matched contributions.

Other Investments

Hedge Fund - an investment fund that is only open to a limited range of wealthy investors that is permitted by regulators to undertake a wider range of investments and trading activities that pays a performance fee to its investment manager. Every hedge fund manager sets the investment strategy and determines the type of investments and the methods of investment it undertakes. Hedge funds invest in a broad range of investments including shares, debt and commodities and they require a large investment of usually a half a million dollars at least. Some very successful ones require more.

The investor needs to keep their money in the account for a specified amount of time and can not withdraw before that time. The manager will set the time to try to fulfill his strategy to make a certain guaranteed return by the maturation date by using a variety of methods, such as short selling and derivatives that have increased risk; with the expectation of increasing the return on investment.

Private Equity - an asset class that consists of equity securities in operating companies that are not publicly traded on a stock exchange, the various types include leveraged buyouts, venture capital, growth capital, distressed investments and mezzanine capital. Capital for private equity is raised mostly from institutional investors and very wealthy individuals. The private equity firm buys a majority of shares in a mature firm or as in venture capital or growth capital they invest in young or emerging companies for 3-5 years at a time and then decide whether to sell out or stage an IPO.

529 Savings Plan – a tax-free account for future college tuition costs, legally referred to as: "qualified tuition plans". They are sponsored by the state, a state agency or educational institutions. The two types are: 1) Pre-paid plan – buy credits for tuition, books, R&B, locks in price, age/grade limits, residency requirements, limited enrollment period 2) College Savings Plan – pay installments, no lock on price, no age limit, no residency requirement, open enrollment, investment options
****
Take what you've learned here and use it, financial

education is what separates the haves from the have nots. Of all that I'm trying to teach you, the following is of tremendous value:

The microcosm of a republic which is a corporation is the greatest way to ascend to the highest level of wealth that can extend to any land on earth. A corporation is a never-ending entity that can make you and your family dynasty unlimited amounts of money. Soldiers of monarchs and emperors used to traipse around the world looking for lands to invade and conquer so that they could take the gold, silver and precious resources of weaker nations. Now the corporate titans run the world through innovation and ingenuity. They don't rape and pillage, they sell the world what it needs and desires and make a fortune in the process. Use your financial education to make it big.

Chapter 10: <u>Start a Family Dynasty</u>

The author assumes that you are sexually aware and wishes not to explain the reproductive characteristics of the human species. Even though he enjoys sex very much and wants you to enjoy it as well, if you are not previously informed please seek this knowledge elsewhere. If you are a teenager of 16 years of age reading this book, I'd like to advice you to hold off on this part of your development until after a time period of growing and learning no less than 5 years in length. For everyone else, please find a person that is your equal that you love with your whole heart (or if your custom is to accept an arranged marriage, do so) and make some babies or adopt some orphans.

If you are in the minority of people who practice polygamy, then (man) find two or three deserving females who love you and you love as well and start your family. The great and mighty Lion who is the King of the Jungle lives in a pride consisting of one male and two females. His counterpart of the Asian continent, the Tiger, has the same family arrangement as the lion. The proud cock crows loudly over his many hens. Nature allows for only the most dominant alpha males to share their seed with more than one mate simultaneously. Babies are the byproduct just the same. The survival of the species is propagated.

The human species has practiced polygamy since the first civilization appeared on the earth. The chief citizen was usually the only person allowed such privilege. Women of exceptional beauty and poise were expected to be added to the King's affection. Very poor peasants hoped to have a daughter admired by the richest and most powerful man in the country or tribe. It was an honor to be lavished with the royal jewels and fine robes of silk. The cherished young beauty lived a life of leisure not experienced by most of the entire populace and she was looked up to by other women.

The wives of royalty also enjoyed an increased level of protection from the hostile world that abuses women physically and sexually way more than men. Armed guards accompany them to outings and guard the entrance to their homes. The children are added to this protection as well and you can imagine how much safer a life this would be compared to the foul things that happen to the average family: child abduction, child molestation, kidnapping of women and young girls to be used as sex slaves, robbery and home invasion.

In the modern world a relationship arrangement of this type could help to extend the family numbers in a way that most others are not even thinking about or allowed to do such as the one child law in China to slow population growth in a billion person country. A King of industry with more than one wife can benefit from an additional household income plus another mother to watch the children without having to pay for childcare. Until there are children added to the family there could be 3 incomes to easily surpass the average combined household income level.

The problems that lead to a 50% divorce rate in America arising from money and infidelity would probably be greatly reduced as a larger household income and the fulfillment of a man's natural desire for more than one woman would be satisfied. But of course this is just an examination of one choice in a truly free society and everyone should have the choice to do whatever suits them best.

Larger families have also had the benefit of more workers for the family business and household chores including farm work. In earlier times it meant a better chance for the name to live on through male heirs and business dealings. Males were the predominate heirs to follow in the father's footsteps, but of course a daughter or son can follow either parent now. The late Aristotle Onassis, son of Socrates, who was married to Jackie Kennedy after the death of J.F.K., trained his only son Alexander to take over his billion dollar international shipping business for him.

When his son died in a tragic accident he was devastated. He attempted to train his daughter Christina to run his business, but she was never really interested in an industrial style enterprise. After his death she passed the responsibilities on to non-family members.

This situation could have been helped if he had had more children. That was the ancients solution to just this type of problem. People like billionaire real estate developer Donald Trump, who followed in his father Fred's footsteps into The Trump Organization, is fortunate to have his son Jr. and his daughter Ivanka who wanted to join him and they happily work for the family business. More children makes sense if you want to start a family dynasty. Multi-wife families made better sense for royal families and tribal chieftains. The peasants, serfs and proletariat have to struggle with every generation, the royals do not. The sharecroppers share in generational poverty, the rich stay rich.

Love is free and people should be free to make their own decisions about a loving arrangement. If you live in a truly free society then No government or dogma is your master so be the master of your own life. Kings have lost their power in most countries in today's world, but the King status is alive and well in the realm of business and enterprise. Your family dynasty could be just a paradigm shift away.

Nature made the King and Queen of the jungle dominant masters of their domain. You are a child of nature as well so whether you live the life of status and dominance or live the life of mediocrity and reticence; the choice is yours. A one female one male family or more than one female with one male family is no sin or crime, it is an invention of nature. With the invention of human conscienceness, human beings became free to make their own choices. So the choices of relationship should be respected on the same principles of individual rights; but of course culture dictates attitudes.

Most definitions of family sound something like this: A family is a household, one's spouse, parents or children. It can also be: descendants of a common ancestor, a tribe, a lineage or a group with some common feature. The benefits of being a part of a family are various: 1) you have people to protect you 2) you have people who care about you 3) you have people to help you in times of need.

Rich people like to co-exist in strong familial units for other reasons. They work with each other and make their businesses stronger because of it. If you and your relatives grow-up with the idea that you co-own properties, businesses, real estate and other income generating assets then your bond is even stronger than playing baseball with your cousins during summer break. The lake house vacation is a nice experience, but it can't compete with making your first million together.

You are probably familiar with the saying: Strength in Numbers. Well there is strength in family as well. These people know you in a way that most other people do not. You share many memories that are completely unknown to even your best friends. There is no doubt about it, the family is a strong institution in most people's lives. Use it to your advantage and avoid the possible pitfalls that could present themselves in expanding your enterprise.

The teaching of your children is a task that is claimed by a lot of different entities, but the parent should be the number one source of information to their children when it comes to formulating their life philosophy and crafting a plan for success. You know how to do it, so teach your children to do it from an early age. Do not waste their minds with lies about fairies, flying saints and other make-believe nonsense.

Give your children the truth about life. Tell them that it is not always fair, but you can have an advantage if you know the Wealth Building Strategies outlined in this publication. The forming of a family dynasty starts with you. The parents are the creators and their children are the keepers of the flame. Don't let your fire flicker out because you did not inform the next generation as to the secrets of success. They will have it better than you. They will have proven methods to choose from to create a most glorious life story.

Give them the keys to the safe and guide them to make their

own decisions using the greatest strategies used by the mega-rich and famous. Nurture their innate talents and let them develop into the person they were meant to be. You have more money so you can let them make mistakes and hold a safety net under them so they won't break their necks from trying to go too hard. Remember to teach them the value of a dollar (insert currency of choice here) and that they may need to work at a lower level when first starting out, but it is only temporary because the cream always rises to the top.

Give them love and respect so that they may give it to others. Parents really are the first molders of the next generation. Feed them garbage and they will become garbage people (garbage in, garbage out), but feed them the most wholesome of nutrients and they grow strong and radiant.

If your children have an interest in your business endeavors then by all means nurture it. But if they don't then tell them that as a family it is each person's responsibility to keep the income generating assets of the family going. If a trust service has to be employed to manage the financial accounts then so be it. Your children can pursue their hearts desires and help watch after the family pot. You must let them be themselves, but instill the sense of duty to the family. They should respect it because it is the source of the family money.

The great John D. Rockefeller of the Standard Oil Co. accumulated his great wealth by realizing that the emerging oil market of the early 20th century would become even more lucrative for the companies that refined the oil which is a necessary step to getting the product to market as gasoline, kerosene and motor oil. He bought out most of his competition with money and shares in his co. This created the largest oil company in the country which eventually was forced by anti-monopoly laws to break-up in 1911 into smaller parts which survive as the main players in the industry today.

Continental Oil became Conoco, which is now a part of ConocoPhillips. Standard Oil of Indiana became Amoco, which is now a part of BP. Standard Oil of California became Chevron. Standard Oil of New Jersey became Esso, which later changed it's name to Exxon, which is now a part of ExxonMobil. Standard Oil of New York became Mobil, which is now a part of ExxonMobil; and Standard Oil of Ohio became Sohio, which is now a part of BP. The Rockefeller family still owns a huge portion of all these assets and many more in banking, shipping, mining, railroads, and real estate.

John D. Rockefeller worked with his son to set-up family trusts and foundations such as the Rockefeller Foundation that have benefited the world in medicine, education, and scientific research. John D. started The University of Chicago and Rockefeller University.

He also built Rockefeller Center in New York City and donated 100s of millions of dollars to schools such as African-American college for women, Spelman College, located in Atlanta that named Rockefeller Hall after him. The name Spelman is in honor of his abolitionists in-laws. He believed in his own ability to succeed and that one should give back to help society. He abstained from alcohol & smoking.

In the 17th century the family that would become the most powerful international banking family in history began to hang a red hexagram in front of their house to identify it. They then decided to take the name red-shield (Rothschild in German) as their surname after the red Seal of Solomon that they used and The Rothschild Family Dynasty was born.

In 1753 Mayer Amschel Rothschild was sent to become a rabbi when he was 10. One year and a half later his parents died. Mayer was encouraged by relatives to continue his studies but coin trading was his true love, so he left the school and when he turned 13 he went to Hanover to become an apprentice at the Oppenheimer bank. He worked there for 7 years, and learned the ins and outs of money. After his apprenticeship to the banking firm of Jakob Wolf Oppenheim in Hamburg, he returned to business in Frankfurt in 1763. At the house at 148 Judengasse (Jewish Alley, {a Ghetto}) in Frankfurt, Germany he set-up his residence and his rare coin dealing business.

Mayer Amschel Rothschild married Guttle Schnapper (1753-1849), the daughter of Wolf Salomon Schnapper, on August 29th, 1770. They had the following children:

Schönche Jeannette Rothschild (August 20, 1771 – 1859) - married Benedikt Moses Worms (1772–1824)
Amschel "Anselm" Mayer (June 12, 1773 – 6 December 1855)
Salomon Mayer (September 9, 1774 – 28 July 1855)
Nathan Mayer (September 16, 1777 – 18 July 1836)
Isabella Rothschild July 2, 1781 – 1861)
Babette Rothschild (August 29, 1784 – 16 March 1869)
Calmann "Carl" Mayer (April 24, 1788 – 10 March 1855)
Julie Rothschild (May 1, 1790 – 19 June 1815)
Henriette (1791–1866) married Abraham Montefiore (1788–1824)
Jacob "James" Mayer (1792–1868)

In a short time, he went from coin dealing to international financing with governments, princes, and kings of Europe throughout the 1800s. He became a dealer in rare coins and won the patronage of Crown Prince Wilhelm of Hesse, and was given the title of "Court Factor". Mayer's coin business grew to include a number of princely customers, and then he expanded into banking services to Crown Prince Wilhelm, who became Wilhelm IX, Landgrave of Hesse-Kassel in 1785. Mayer's business expanded rapidly following the French Revolution when he handled the payments between Great Britain and Hesse for the hire of Hessian mercenaries.

His five sons took up the family business and expanded it by each relocating to the biggest and most major European capitals. Salomon set-up a branch in Vienna, Austria, Nathan set-up a branch in London, England, Jacob set-up a branch in Paris, France, Calmann set-up a branch in Naples, Italy, and his eldest son Amschel took over the original Frankfort, Germany branch after his father's death. By using their own secret intelligence service and their own private courier system which was faster than the regular mail they could get political or economic news that they used to outmaneuver European governments. They all married women picked by their father for family connections.

The Rothschild family have interests in not only banking, but also trading, manufacturing plants, mines, hotels, gold, and real estate all over the world. Baron Edmond de Rothschild – (1845-1934) was very instrumental in the establishment of Israel. His money paid to drain swamps, dig wells and build houses. It founded industries such as scent factories, glass works, wine cellars and bottle manufacturers. His trust funds paid for Hebrew University, the promotion of education, science and culture and he is known as Hanadiv' (the Hebrew word for 'benefactor') throughout Palestine.

The modern family has connections to Compagnie Financlere, which is a holding company in France, Banque Privee in Switzerland, Banque Lambert, Isrop, which controls the Israel General Bank, Israel Corporation, Tri-Continental Pipelines, Shell, New Court, Bank of France, Bank of England, Federal Reserve of N.Y. and DeBeers Consolidated Mines in South Africa just to name a few.

They meet with the Bilderbergers, the Tri-Lateral Commission and The First International Bank of Israel is located at 39 Rothschild Boulevard in Tel Aviv. Their investments are too numerous to name without being an agent of the family or a member yourself. From the humble beginnings with coin dealing in the racially segregated German ghetto, the dynasty of the House Of Rothschild became the richest banking family business in history.

Instill that sense of duty in your children and it will be like *you* cloned yourself. Success will come with sheer determination and an open mind. Remember the earlier statements that I made about being free? Now do you see why it is a chief necessity in wealth building? Always keep your mind free and open. Stay free of excessive alcohol drinking (Don't drink or smoke), stay free from narcotic drug use and stay free from fools that have been trained to be average. Remain free and clear of unnatural foods and drinks. Find your path and your family will help you if they know your reasonings are just.

Your strength, your determination and intelligence will

reflect it's light onto your satellites: Your Children. Be the SUN in their lives and shine your light of wisdom upon them. They will love you for making them work for a living though rich beyond most people's wildest dreams because laziness is just not acceptable in a respectable house. You have built a foundation, let your children build the rest. Let them take the house and make it a palace.

Not just children bring the family dynasty into being; siblings can spark the flame as well. Warner Bros. was founded in 1918 by Jewish immigrants from Poland when the brothers opened the Warner Bros. studio on Sunset Boulevard in Hollywood. Sam and Jack Warner produced the pictures, while Harry and Albert Warner and their auditor and controller Paul Ashley Chase handled finance and distribution in New York City. They incorporated as Warner Brothers Pictures, Inc in 1923.

They were responsible for the first successful "talkie", The Jazz Singer; and the Lights of New York caused all the studios to abandon silent films for good. The co. put out such classics as the Public Enemy, Casablanca, Gypsy, A street car named Desire, Bonnie & Clyde, the Harry Potter series and a ton more produced, co-produced, distributed and acquired films and tv shows.

Warner Bros. is the third-oldest major American film studio in continuous operation. It is currently a subsidiary of Time Warner, with its headquarters in Burbank, California and New York City. Warner Bros. has several subsidiary companies, including Warner Bros. Studios, Warner Bros. Pictures, Warner Bros. Records, Warner Bros. Books, Warner Bros. Interactive Entertainment, Warner Bros. Television, Warner Bros. Animation, Warner

Home Video, New Line Cinema, TheWB.com and DC Comics. Warner Bros. also owns half of The CW Television Network.

Live the dream, your name will live on forever. Your brand will be greater than you ever imagined. Your life will be an inspiration to all who wish to have a fortunate son or daughter. Do not let it die with you. The human consciousness should never die, we just haven't figured out how to keep it alive yet. Someday in the near future it will be commonplace. Until then, we write, sing and make videos in a crude attempt to live forever; so give it all to your progeny. You have truly made it, you are a made man or woman now. Bestow the grace and power on the genes of your loins, the fruit of your labors, and the beneficiaries of all your love.

Love is the most important reason to share this gift. No one needs any other one. So take the jewels you have been given and let them sparkle. Gems of wisdom can be the most simple statement from a seemingly unlikely source. For example, a children's book author wrote many popular books throughout his life that have been made into cartoon and live action movies and enjoyed by millions. Almost no one thinks about what a great impact his words could have on their little ones, but they should because as I said before early childhood teachings can have a tremendous impact upon you.

Theodor Seuss Geisel, better known as Dr. Seuss said these words:

You have brains in your head. You have feet in your shoes. You can steer yourself

in any direction you choose. You're on your own.
And you know what you know. You are
the guy who'll decide where to go.

Teach your children well, that is the true role of a parent,
not just the biological act of procreation. You may not live
to see the great house rising over the horizon, but it will rise
just as the sun appears to rise over the horizon everyday.
The earth will turn and we will be cast into the darkness of
the shadow of the sun, but we will see the light again. Your
light will Shine on through your Family Dynasty and the
world will celebrate the glory of your triumph forever and
ever.

Chapter 11:   <u>Keep it in the Family</u>

For centuries and centuries and millenniums the royal family has passed on the family jewels to the next generation. The family house has stayed in the family by inheritance to the next of kin and the extended relatives. This system has served them well with little need to revise it over the years. You understand how it goes. The patriarch or matriarch dies and leaves the house to the eldest and gives money and other possessions to the children and grandchildren. Everyone is enriched by the process and the family as a whole is made richer because of it.

Many scams have been devised over the centuries to prevent this system from taking place amongst poor and middle class families. It has worked with many different methods. The example stated earlier from the Egyptians about the need to have worldly possessions buried with you has been modified in modern times to include the need to help charities and heathens in third world countries. Your own relatives are left holding the bag when it comes to your burial expenses and debts, but less fortunates are given handouts with your life savings and life insurance payouts.

There is no harm in helping others, but why must you burden your own family in the process? Of course you should give the majority of your worldly possessions to your relatives. Why would you not want them to have a better life more than complete strangers that may have contributed to their own poverty or homelessness? Give no more than 10% to less fortunates, do not fall for the scams of some non-profit organizations used to fleece elderly people out of their life's savings and property.

Keeping yourself and your family safe may seem like a non issue to you, but when you're rich you have to be more sure of safety then everyone else. While yes it is true that poor people are usually the most common people to be victims of violence because of their tendency to live in poorer quality neighborhoods; wealthy people have more to protect. They are targets of criminals and loonies so you should prepare yourself with every possible safeguard.

In the times of knights sponsored by the King, the protection of the kingdom was maintained by brave and courageous men. They wore ironclad plates shaped from their bodies to keep themselves from being sliced and stabbed by the swords of their enemies. Wearing suits of armor made their fight a valiant contest of skill between each combatant that sometimes ended in death. But the good guys usually outlasted the bad guys because they were sponsored by the monarchy which could afford to spare no expense to arm it's soldiers with the very best gear.

Fast forward to the modern times. Police officers wear blue cotton and polyester blend uniforms. They carry handguns, a billy club, handcuffs and sometimes a stun gun or taser. The bad guys carry knives, semi-automatic handguns, sawed-off shotguns, semi-automatic rifles and assault rifles if they can get their hands on them. They have access to bulletproof vests and armor piercing hollowpoint bullets. When the bad guys shoot at a cop and hit, they kill them easily. The cops don't usually wear bulletproof vests so they die much more easily than their ancient counterparts the noble knights.

Why did this happen? Did people forget that the life of a

knight can be ended if you don't wear the proper protection? I can't say for sure, but I know this: Common people stopped using common sense. Everyone mourns and celebrates the life of a slain hero of the police department when they die in the line of duty. But the question is: Did they really have to die? Because they shouldn't be going into war without a suit of armor. It only makes sense to protect yourself appropriately. You have to keep yourself safe proportionally to the level of danger that exists in your life.

The kings did not send their knights out to fight in cotton pants and cotton shirts and you can not protect yourself against the jackals who will want to take your riches from you either without the proper safeguards. Think like a king, not like a pauper.

Make sure to install a security system in your house, your cars and other vehicles. Install fire and carbon monoxide detectors and sprinklers to protect yourself from fire. Use buildings made of brick, steel, concrete blocks, stone, and earthen materials because they don't burn as easily as wood and aluminum sliding. Keep insurance on your house with fire and flood protection, and on your other personal property as well.

Keep jewelry in a safe or safedeposit box and use filing cabinets for your important documents. If you need to feel even more safe, there is a service you can get done for maximum surety. You can have bulletproof windows put in on your house and your car can be bulletproofed for about $50,000. It could save your life or that of your loved ones or guests.

A monitoring service such as ADT could alert the police or fire department for you. The OnStar service for cars by GM can guide you with GPS, stop a car thief by disabling your car and it can call the police if you're in an accident. A small price to pay to keep your family safe. *With great wealth comes great responsibility to protect it.*

You could equip your cars with ride-flat tires to avoid having to change a flat in a bad neighborhood. And of course you could hire a security person to accompany you or your relatives on their excursions. Staying in a gated community with a guard on duty to key acceptable people in or building your own compound with these same characteristics is a rich people staple. They do it to stay safe. You should do it too. Paparazzi can be deterred from stalking you and trying to get unflattering or private moment pictures as well if you use these precautions.

Keep it in the family by employing an attorney to draft a trust fund to keep the bulk of your plus million dollar estate from going to federal estate taxes after your demise. Give your possessions away to your children before you die or to a family foundation. There are tax benefits from this, consult your attorney, tax expert or accountant for current laws because they change frequently.

I looked up the word Pedestrian in a thesaurus; this is what I got as a response: artless, banal, blah, blank, bloodless, boring, characterless, colorless, commonplace, dead, dim, dismal, dreary, dry, dull, empty, flat, hollow, humdrum, inane, inapt, inexcitable, insipid, lifeless, mediocre, monotone, monotonous, mundane, ordinary, plain, pointless, poor, spiritless, stale, sterile, stodgy, superficial, tasteless, unembellished, unimaginative, unimpassioned, uninspired, unromantic, unskillful, and vapid. If this is the way your life is defined then don't listen to any of my advice, this is not for you. But if you know who you are and what you are then take it all in and keep it in the family.

Charity starts at home and education starts at home also. You wanted to learn the real deal of becoming a wealthy person and thats what I gave you. No B.S., no fantasies such as sitting on one's ass collecting checks from no effort put in like the poor people pipe dreams. Even the state lottery requires you to go to the store and invest at least one dollar to win. **There is always an investment at the source of success**; believe it or disbelieve it at your own peril. As you Think you will Grow Rich if you know the right things to think about and then take action. Nothing will happen without action.

The Law Of Attraction always attracts that which you desire with all your heart and mind. That is why people in a very negative space keep seeing crime everyday and stay in poverty. They see it, they complain about it and they keep seeing it again and again. It's what they focus on, while the prosperous person is focused on becoming better and wealthier everyday. You can only attract that which you focus on into your life. So quit complaining about not having enough money and start focusing on how to get more money coming in: better job, income generating assets, spending less.

But please don't read into my statements about what you focus on gets you what happens in your life. Unlike other writers on this subject; I do not believe that if you are sick or suffering then it's because you asked for it. That is nonsense. I am saying that you will have a random, unfulfilling life if you do not use the Law of Attraction, but it won't make you a cancer patient. That is a cruel and despicable interpretation. Some illness is defined as psychosomatic, but only a doctor can determine that for sure, not Rhonda Byrne – and that's NO *Secret*. Yes, I do believe that sometimes sh*t happens and it's not your fault and other people's actions cause you harm without you wanting it to happen.

All I'm saying is: If you don't try to get what you want out of life then you will probably not get what you want. Life is never totally within your control, because you can't control other people's actions. But you can effect some of what happens to you by what you focus on; so think appropriately.

Chapter 12: <u>Resources</u>

The information contained in this book was lovingly compiled to help you get to where you want to be. It was written with the intention to teach you a better way to obtain your goals. Because of the ever changing world that we live in it was not possible or it was deemed to not be wise to list resources in the back of the book, but put new and updated contact info on a website. So that's what we did. Since you made it this far why not keep going until you reach that goal that you set? I would love to know that I helped at least one person to become the best person they can be.

Go to: <u>www.WealthBuildingStrategies.org</u> and click on Log-in. You will be prompted to type in a Username and Password. The **Username is: Customer** and the **Password is: IamWealthy**. Please do not share this with anyone else. The site is for people who have read the book and understand <u>The 9 Greatest Strategies for Building Wealth</u>. As you read in the Implement the Strategies chapter, you have to research the particular tasks you need to perform to accomplish your plan for success. We have found some links of organizations that can help.

Everything has not been laid out for you on this website, however; it is very important that you learn to think for yourself and make your own choices. We have tried to assist you with info about companies and government agencies that provide assistance to people who are striving for betterment and self-improvement. I hope you will find it very useful and I thank-you for your purchase of my very first book. It was an eye-opening experience and I learned just as much as you have.

Or at least I learned as much as I hope you gained from it. The process required me to research some of the richest and most successful people in history. I enjoyed reading through all the quotes from successful and deep-thinking people that I found. So many wise words have been said that it was considerably time consuming trying to decide on which ones to include. I believe the inclusion of other people's opinions makes this publication much better than just being my opinion only. I am not the smartest man who has ever lived and I am not ashamed to say that greatness comes from wisdom.

Wise people have lived through tough times and they have studied and learned well. Everyone has something they can learn from the accomplishments and failures of others. No need to *try everything once* as the saying goes (trying something stupid once could end your one and only life); learn from your own mistakes and someone else's too. It is like having a couple more lifetimes of knowledge to guild you. Never underestimate the power of knowledge. Never underestimate the benefit of wisdom. Hear every lesson when it is being told and give lessons back to everyone you can.

Use the resources on www.WealthBuildingStrategies.org and make your dreams come true. Dreams are the sparks, but waking up and accomplishing is the flame. Follow your plan for success. Use the wealth building strategies of the super rich to start your family dynasty.

Chapter 13:   <u>About the Author</u>

I was born Lionel L. White in S. Eastern Virginia on August 4th , same day as President Obama. I live in Virginia Beach,Va. From an early age I've had a great love for music of all kinds, but especially rock music from the 60s, 70s and the 90s. I also listen to R&B, funk, pop, classical and hip hop. I loved singing with the radio as a young child, and started writing songs and poetry at age 12 and messing around on a toy keyboard. At age 13 I began learning to play the trumpet which I continued to do until the 10th grade when I switched to playing the tuba. I quit band after the 11th grade when my high school, Salem H.S., won the state title for concert band and came in 2nd for marching band.

Around age 14 I became enamored with the rap style of lyric and I wrote voraciously and joined a rap group at 16. The group played shows around the S. Eastern Virginia area and cut demos with local producers and even met with Timbaland, who was still Djing, to listen to some of his first tracks before he became famous. We opened up a show at Norfolk State University in October 1991 where The Leaders of the New School performed. I lost interest in the group about a year or so later because of my intense desire to create my own (www.LucianoIlluminati.com) music and not sample music.

I started playing guitar at age 20 and eventually bought enough recording equipment to make home recordings. I played in a funk rock band for a few years. I experimented with different sounds and mixes for many years until I finally finished a demo CD called Royal Jelly in the summer of 1999. For a year and a half the local girls and college girls came to the restaurant where I worked at on the Va Beach oceanfront to smile and show their bikini-clad breast to me so much that the owner was very annoyed with the obvious flirtation. I continued on making my Rock & Rhythm music and working in music production in the local area until 2003 when I started to pursue other interests.

In 2003 I was surrounded by beautiful females at Old Dominion University that inspired my new interest in the words on t-shirts business. I started to draft a few logo designs that I later put on the shelf to focus on a computer-based business centering on the internet. My first company was called SmartPeopleOrderItOnline Inc. founded in Feb. 2007. I started SPOIO Inc. in December 2008 with a multi-tiered structure that consists of online properties: www.SPOIO.com - Discount SuperStore which sells over 1 million products in the following categories: electronics, computers, sports, home & garden, flowers, jewelry, toys & games, cell phones, health & beauty, apparel, auto, and more.

SPOIO Wireless (www.SPOIO.net) – a wireless service directory with phones and service by verizon, at&t, t-mobile, alltel, sprint and nextel. Most phones are delivered free by FedEx and there are many free phone offers when you start a new contract. www.SPOIO.info is the news & info site with Google Search. www.2FSex.com is the sex health and enhancement site. SPOIO Publishing is the publishing imprint and Luciano Illuminati Clothing is the first product of the apparel division.

I decided that I would write a book after starting my

publishing division, so in August of 2009 I did just that. This book only took me about 2 and a half months to complete, but I feel that it is very wise and deep. I plan to continue my singing career, writing and running SPOIO Inc. as well. Best Wishes!

Appendix

A: Jobs and Income Survey..................................119

B: Super Rich People who used the Strategies.....127

C: Most Profitable Industries..............................131

D: Most Profitable Companies............................139

E: Assets and Liabilities of Households..............148

F: More Great Quotes..151

Appendix A: <u>Jobs and Income Survey</u>

You need to know which jobs pay the most money to be able to make a good judgment as to what you should do with your life. The following list will give you a good idea as to what type of income you can expect to make and give you an idea of what other people are making. It will be an eye opening experience. People choose what they want in life partly by choosing their career. Remember the words to that poem by Jesse Rittenhouse that you read earlier, make sure you ask LIFE for the type of income that you want. If you want more than average then don't choose an average income.

Or be prepared to implement some of the other strategies besides working for oneself such as stock investment where you have your money working for you. Remember that there is no one way, you can achieve wealth any way you want to. I've compiled a list from The U.S. Bureau of Labor Statistics' National Compensation Survey for 2009. First you will be presented with info on the gathering of info and the number of employees polled for the survey. The survey begins on page 125.

Knowledge from stats is how managers make educated decisions, you too should think like a portfolio manager because the numbers never lie. But these numbers may start to tell lies to people who read this survey in a few years, so make sure you keep up with the newest version of the survey by going to: www.BLS.gov. The National Compensation Survey is conducted about every 3 years.

Source: U.S. Bureau of Labor Statistics, National
Compensation Survey

National Compensation Survey:

Occupational Wages in the
United States, June 2008
U.S. Department of Labor
U.S. Bureau of Labor Statistics
December 2007 - January 2009

Technical Note
The data in this report are based on the National
Compensation Survey (NCS) conducted by the U.S. Bureau
of Labor Statistics (BLS). The NCS is locality based and
covers establishments in private industry and State and
local governments. Agriculture, private households, and the
Federal Government are excluded from the scope of the
survey.

Survey scope. The 2008 NCS included establishments
representing approximately 128 million workers within the
scope of the survey. (See Appendix table 1.)
Establishments with one or more workers are covered in the
survey. For purposes of this survey, an establishment is an
economic unit that produces goods or services, a central
administrative office, or an auxiliary unit providing support
services to a company.

For private industries in this survey, the establishment is
usually at a single physical location. For State and local
governments, an establishment is defined as all locations of
a government entity. The employment figures reflect for the
first time poststratification, to adjust survey sample weights

to reflect current employment by industry. See the article at **www.bls.gov/opub/cwc/cm20070122ar01p1.htm** for more information.

Sampling frame. The list of establishments from which the survey sample was selected (sampling frame) was developed from State unemployment insurance reports. The reference month for the public sector is June 1994. Due to the volatility of industries within the private sector, sampling frames were developed using the most recent month of reference available at the time the sample was selected. The reference month for the private sector varied by area. ***Sample design.*** The sample for this survey was selected using a 3-stage design.

The first stage involved the selection of areas. The NCS sample consists of 152 metropolitan areas and nonmetropolitan areas that represent the Nation's 326 metropolitan statistical areas (as defined by the U.S. Office of Management and Budget) and the remaining portions of the 50 States.

Metropolitan areas are defined as Metropolitan Statistical Areas (MSAs) or Consolidated Metropolitan Statistical Areas (CMSAs), as defined by the Office of Management and Budget in 1994. Nonmetropolitan areas are counties that do not fit the metropolitan area definition. In the second stage, the sample of establishments was drawn by first stratifying the sampling frame by ownership and industry.

Number of workers1 represented by the survey, United States, June 2008[2]

Occupational group	Civilian workers	Private industry workers	State and local government workers
All workers	128000000	109520000	18478700
Management, professional, and related	34092700	24509500	9583300
Management, business, and financial	9916400	8528700	1387700
Professional and related	24176300	15980700	8195600
Service	26592700	22386200	4206500
Sales and office	34143500	31354200	2789300
Sales and related	12857900	12790000	67900
Office and administrative support	21285600	18564200	2721400
Natural resources, construction, and maintenance	11921700	10908800	1012900
Construction and extraction	6642000	6090000	551900
Installation, maintenance, and repair	5120300	4676200	444100

Occupational group	Civilian workers	Private industry workers	State and local government workers
Production, transportation, and material moving	21249600	20362800	886800
Production	10467800	10297600	170100
Transportation and material moving	10781800	10065100	716700

1) The number of workers represented by the survey are rounded to the nearest 100. Estimates of the number of workers provide a description of size and composition of the labor force included in the survey. Estimates are not intended, however, for comparison to other statistical series to measure employment trends or levels.
2) The survey covers all 50 states and the District of Columbia. Data were collected between December 2007 and January 2009. The average month of reference was June 2008.
3) Workers are classified by occupation using the 2000 Standard Occupational Classification (SOC) system.

NOTE: Dashes indicate that no data were reported or that data did not meet publication criteria.

SOURCE: Bureau of Labor Statistics,
National Compensation Survey

1) Employees are classified as working either a full-time or a part-time schedule based on the definition used by each establishment. Therefore, a worker with a 35-hour-per-week schedule might be considered a full-time employee in one establishment, but classified as part-time in another firm, where a 40-hour week is the minimum full-time schedule.

2) A classification system including about 800 individual occupations is used to cover all workers in the civilian economy.

3) Earnings are the straight-time hourly wages or salaries paid to employees. They include incentive pay, cost-of-living adjustments, and hazard pay. Excluded are premium pay for overtime, vacations, and holidays; nonproduction bonuses; and tips. The mean is computed by totaling the pay of all workers and dividing by the number of workers, weighed by hours.

4) Mean weekly earnings are the straight-time weekly wages or salaries paid to employees. Median weekly earnings designate position – one-half of the earnings are paid the same as or more than the rate shown and half are paid the same as or less than the rate shown. Mean weekly hours are the hours an employee is scheduled to work in a week, exclusive of overtime.

5) Mean annual earnings are the straight-time annual wages or salaries paid to employees. Median annual earnings designate position – one-half of the earnings are paid the same as or more than the rate shown and half are paid the same as or less than the rate shown. Mean annual hours are the hours an employee is scheduled to work in a year, exclusive of overtime.

Jobs and Income Survey of 2009

Occupation	Hrly Erngs Mean | Median	Wkly Hrs	Annual Erngs Mean | Median
All workers .... 21.90 | 17.50		39.6	44,101 | 35,861
Management occupations 43.60 | 38.82		40.6	91,404 | 81,313
Chief executives .... 106.53 | 69.47		43.5	241,065 | 162,499
General and operations managers .... 48.00 | 40.10		41.7.	104,086 | 89,997
Legislators .... 27.82 | 27.69		34.6	50,000 | 49,948
Advertising and promotions managers .... 35.58 | 32.30		41.1	75,986 | 69,056
Marketing and sales .... 47.66 | 43.43		40.8	101,087 | 91,374
managers			
Marketing managers .... 49.73 | 46.81		40.0	103,454 | 96,100
Sales managers .... 45.48 | 41.25		41.6	98,478 | 86,507
Public relations managers ...41.88 | 35.70		39.6	86,294 | 73,117
Administrative services managers .... 33.78 | 31.49		40.4	70,781 | 66,321
Computer and information systems managers .... 54.01 | 51.92		40.3	113,226 | 107,543
Financial managers .... 44.96 | 39.35		40.5	94,551 | 83,500
Human resources managers .41.20 | 38.94		40.1	85,799 | 80,725
Compensation and benefits managers .... 36.45 | 33.86		40.6	76,907 | 73,100
Training and development managers .... 40.81 | 34.62		40.1	85,165 | 72,001
Industrial production managers .... 42.29 | 41.57		40.7	89,579 | 86,792
Purchasing managers .... 43.67 | 39.09		40.3	91,498 | 81,313
Transportation, storage, and distribution managers .... 38.41 | 35.70		40.4	80,577 | 73,723
Agricultural managers .... 29.63 | 23.39		40.0	61,639 | 48,651
Farm, ranch, and other agricultural managers .... 31.30 | 23.39		40.0	65,107 | 48,651
Construction managers .... 37.01 | 36.06		40.9	78,638 | 75,837
Education administrators .... 39.46 | 37.71		39.6	76,287 | 72,055
Education administrators,			

Occupation	Hrly Erngs Mean | Median	Wkly Hrs	Annual Erngs Mean | Median
preschool and child care center/program	23.44 | 22.78	40.4	48,124 | 44,054
Education administrators, elementary and secondary school	45.79 | 45.14	39.6	84,833 | 81,885
Education administrators, postsecondary	40.08 | 34.92	39.0	80,471 | 70,264
Engineering managers	55.80 | 56.02	40.6	117,884 | 119,407
Food service managers	25.65 | 23.22	44.2	58,527 | 51,840
Funeral directors	24.39 | 20.37	41.4	52,484 | 45,001
Lodging managers	24.71 | 18.88	42.5	54,579 | 43,680
Medical and health services managers	39.48 | 35.82	40.7	83,094 | 73,944
Natural sciences managers .	44.71 | 41.48	39.6	92,067 | 86,276
Property, real estate, and community association managers	26.18 | 23.82	40.0	54,388 | 49,539
Social and community service managers	27.36 | 25.15	39.5	56,157 | 51,524

The Abridged Version only contains information about the managerial positions. If you would like more stats then purchase the full version of Wealth Building Strategies of the Super Rich: How to Start a Family Dynasty or GO TO: www.BLS.gov.

Appendix B: <u>Super Rich People who used the Strategies</u>

Every single person on this list is a billionaire, the exact amount of their fortune is not included due to the fluctuating nature of high net worth individuals who own stock which can change in value daily, weekly, and monthly. The purpose of this appendix is to give you examples of each of <u>The 9 Greatest Strategies for Building Wealth</u> at work in the real world. You should look them up if you'd like more details about how they made their fortunes. These people will undoubtedly continue to be wealthy for the rest of their lives and pass on their wealth and knowledge to their family dynasty.

<u>Bill Gates</u> (1,5,6) – co-founder of Microsoft Corporation, former CEO of Microsoft and current Chairman

<u>Warren Buffett</u> (1,5,6) – CEO of Berkshire Hathaway, full-time investor

<u>Larry Ellison</u> (1,5,6) – founder of Oracle, CEO of Oracle

<u>Ingvar Kamprad</u> (1,5,6) – founder of Ikea furniture co.

<u>Maria Aramburuzabala</u> (1,8) – investor in Grupo Modelo, the maker of Corona and Negro Modelo beers

<u>Sergey Brin</u> (1,5,6) – co-founder of Google search engine internet company, Pres. of Technology @ Google

Larry Page (1,5,6) – co-founder of Google search engine internet company, Pres. of Products @ Google

David Rockefeller Sr. (1,6,8) - Standard Oil stock inheritance (now ExxonMobil, Chevron, BP, Amoco and ConocoPhilips; as well as banking and other interests)

William Wrigley (1,6,8) – Wrigley chewing gum company

Lee Shau Kee (1,2,6) – real estate development, CEO Henderson Land Development

Donald J. Trump (1,2,3,5,6,7,8) – real estate, property management; author, tv show, CEO The Trump Organization

Steven Spielberg (1,3,5,6) – movie director and producer, founded Amblin Entertainment, co-founded DreamWorks

George Lucas (1,3,5,6) – movie director, producer and screenwriter, founded LucasFilms and Industrial Light & Magic special effects company

Oprah Winfrey (1,3,5,6,7) – talk show host, actor, and author; founded Harpo production company

Tiger Woods (1,4,6,7) - the world's 1st sports competitor to receive a billionaire dollars total career income

J.K. Rowling (1,5,6) - author of the Harry Potter series, full-time writer, first billionaire writer

Paul McCartney (1,3,5,7) – may or may not still be a

billionaire since his divorce from Heather Mills, but with all the new Beatles stuff coming out all the time such as The Beatles Rock Band video game and a new remastered version of most of their music released on 9-9-09, it's only a matter of time.

Peter Buck PhD (1,6) – co-founded Subway restaurant chain; Doctor's Associates

Fame is a contributor to all wealth building so there is no one person or brand to represent it, here are a few well-known billion dollar names: L'oreal, Coca-Cola, Nike, McDonald's, Hilton, Macy's, Apple

Jim, Alice, Helen, S. Robson and Christy Walton (1,2,6,8) – all received inheritances from their relative Sam Walton, the founder of Walmart Stores which owns Walmart, Sam's Club and other stores

There are no billionaire gamblers but the people who own the casinos definitely make sure the house always wins: Sheldon Adelson, and Stephen Wynn among others are billionaire casino owners

There are many more examples of The 9 Greatest Strategies for Building Wealth working for many other billionaires and millionaires throughout the world, it would make no sense to list any more here. These strategies work is all that you need take away from this little list. Read Forbes magazine's special issue on billionaires for a more indepth list and read it regularly for good business info. Also BusinessWeek, The Wall Street Journal and Investors Business Daily are excellent as well.

Be inspired to live your dreams or be nothing; the choice is yours. Some people believe that there are only two types of people: Somebodies and Nobodies. So make yourself a somebody, that's an order. That is the purpose of my writing this book. If I haven't enlightened anybody to choose to become someone great then I've failed and I don't like to fail, so re-read this book as often as necessary to achieve total comprehension.

You can get listed by Forbes if you put forth all the effort and creativity that you can muster. There is no difference between the wealthy people listed and you. You just haven't received your fortune yet, but it's coming. If you keep the faith then you know it's coming. Super rich people are people who know The 9 Greatest Strategies for Building Wealth and use them.

Appendix C: Most Profitable Industries

Number of Tax Returns, Receipts, and Net Income by Type of Business and Industry: 2005

[**21,468 represents 21,468,000**. Covers active enterprises only. Figures are estimates based on sample of unaudited tax returns. Based on the North American Industry Classification System (NAICS), 2002; see text, this section] Industry **2002**

Industries	NAI CS code	Number of returns (1,000)			Business receipts 1 (bil. Dol.)			Net income (less loss) (bil. Dol.)		
		Nonfarm proprietor-ships | Partnerships | Corpo-rations |			Nonfarm proprietor-ships | Partnerships | Corpo-rations |			Nonfarm proprietor-ships | Partnerships | Corpo-rations |		
Total	(X)	21468	2764	5,671	1223	3719	24,060	270	546	1,949
Agriculture, forestry, fishing, and hunting 2	11	268	128	142	16	23	126	1	2	5

Industries	NAICS code	Number of returns (1,000)			Business receipts 1 (bil. Dol.)			Net income (less loss) (bil. Dol.)		
		Nonfarm proprietorships	Partnerships	Corporations	Nonfarm proprietorships	Partnerships	Corporations	Nonfarm proprietorships	Partnerships	Corporations
Mining	21	121	28	33	11	84	280	2	34	47
Utilities	22	11	3	8	(Z)	162	604	(Z)	3	21
Construction	23	2,821	182	752	222	276	1,427	35	27	74
Special trade contractors	238	2,235	66	454	149	48	575	26	3	22
Manufacturing	31–33	340	45	278	25	705	6,506	3	50	680
Wholesale and retail trade 3	(X)	(NA)	190	993	(NA)	753	6,652	(NA)	17	215
Wholesale trade	42	348	48	374	46	437	3,289	5	13	106
Retail trade 4	44–45	2,474	142	616	197	316	3,362	9	4	109
Motor vehicle and parts dealers	441	159	19	94	41	107	836	1	1	11

Industries	NAICS code	Number of returns (1,000)			Business receipts 1 (bil. Dol.)			Net income (less loss) (bil. Dol.)		
		Nonfarm proprietorships | Partnerships | Corporations |			Nonfarm proprietorships | Partnerships | Corporations |			Nonfarm proprietorships | Partnerships | Corporations |		
Food and beverage stores	445	108	17	97	29	55	498	1	3	13
Gasoline stations	447	39	26	53	20	7	241	(Z)	1	2
Transportation and warehousing	48–49	1,043	42	187	73	93	659	10	6	19
Information 4	51	335	37	123	9	200	887	2	26	75
Broadcasting (except Internet)	515	551	2	6	52	35	107	5(Z)	3	5
Telecommunications	517	(5)	4	18	(5)	118	389	(5)	16	26
Finance and insurance	52	706	288	243	72	447	3,302	19	198	501

Industries	NAICS code	Number of returns (1,000)			Business receipts 1 (bil. Dol.)			Net income (less loss) (bil. Dol.)		
		Nonfarm proprietor-ships	Partnerships	Corpo-rations	Nonfarm proprietor-ships	Partnerships	Corpo-rations	Nonfarm proprietor-ships	Partnerships	Corpo-rations
Real estate and rental and leasing	53	1,350	1,296	642	83	285	268	33	72	30
Professional, scientific, and technical services 4	54	2,883	170	786	145	267	814	61	67	31
Legal services	5411	338	27	104	38	115	83	16	42	8
Accounting, tax preparation, bookkeep-ing, and payroll scrvices.	5412	356	20	67	12	43	35	5	9	3

Industries	NAICS code	Number of returns (1,000)			Business receipts 1 (bil. Dol.)			Net income (less loss) (bil. Dol.)		
		Nonfarm proprietorships | Partnerships | Corporations |			Nonfarm proprietorships | Partnerships | Corporations |			Nonfarm proprietorships | Partnerships | Corporations |		
Management, scientific, and technical consulting services	5416	763	43	226	35	36	164	18	7	12
Management of companies and enterprises	55	(NA)	25	51	(NA)	46	895	(NA)	16	161
Administrative and support and waste management and remediation services	56	1,916	48	258	52	61	431	14	5	23
Educational services	61	552	11	45	7	4	33	2	(Z)	3

Industries	NAICS code	Number of returns (1,000)			Business receipts 1 (bil. Dol.)			Net income (less loss) (bil. Dol.)		
		Nonfarm proprietorships	Partnerships	Corporations	Nonfarm proprietorships	Partnerships	Corporations	Nonfarm proprietorships	Partnerships	Corporations
Health care and social assistance	62	1,769	60	381	107	131	515	43	19	27
Arts, entertainment, and recreation	71	1,157	49	116	27	39	80	6	(Z)	4
Accommodation and food services	72	392	96	287	43	124	396	1	3	28
Food services and drinking places	722	336	64	254	38	68	314	1	2	19
Other services 4	81	2,559	62	345	82	20	184	20	1	6
Auto repair and maintenance	8111	338	19	1 06	23	7	64	3	(Z)	2

Industries	NAICS code	Number of returns (1,000)			Business receipts 1 (bil. Dol.)			Net income (less loss) (bil. Dol.)		
		Nonfarm proprietorships | Partnerships | Corporations |			Nonfarm proprietorships | Partnerships | Corporations |			Nonfarm proprietorships | Partnerships | Corporations |		
Personal and laundry services	812	1,488	32	140	38	9	75	11	(Z)	2
Religious, grantmaking, civic, professional, and similar organizations	813	244	1	40	4	(Z)	10	2	(Z)	(Z)
Unclassified	(X)	423	4	3	4	(Z)	(Z)	2	(Z)	(Z)

NA = Not available X = Not applicable Z = Less than $500 million 1 = Includes investment income for partnerships and corporations in finance and insurance, real estate, and management of companies' industries. Excludes investment income for S corporations. 2 = For corporations, represents agricultural services only. 3 = For corporations, includes trade business not identified as wholesale or retail. 4 = Includes other industries not shown separately. 5 = Broadcasting includes telecommunications.

Source: U.S. Internal Revenue Service, *Statistics of Income,* various publications.

Appendix D: <u>Most Profitable Companies</u>

By now I'm sure you have discovered that stock investment is the best way to build wealth. Valuations for publicly traded companies change frequently so you must keep abreast of these fluctuations by reading prospectuses, newsletters such as Investors Business Daily or their website: Investors.com, using online brokers, full-service brokers and financial news aggregators. Consider such things as dividends payout history, assets, market values, debts and profits and future plans before investing in a company. Common sense can be very powerful --- use it.

The following is a listing of some of the most profitable companies in the world, all of these companies make billions in profit every year. Use this list as a guide for further research of the best investments to make the most money on your ROI. Forbes Magazine prints a Global 200 top companies list every year. Starting with the biggest winners is a much better strategy then wild predictions of 500% returns in 6 months that some unscrupulous brokers will make about upstarts just to make a commission. Invest 80% of your money on winners, invest only 20% on wild cards.

<u>Most Profitable Companies Publicly-traded on stock exchanges 2009</u>

<u>Company</u>   <u>Country</u>   <u>Industry</u>
ExxonMobil - United States - Oil & Gas Operations

Gazprom - Russia - Oil & Gas Operations

Company   Country   Industry
Royal Dutch Shell - Netherlands - Oil & Gas Operations

Chevron - United States - Oil & Gas Operations

BP - United Kingdom - Oil & Gas Operations

PetroChina - China - Oil & Gas Operations

General Electric - United States - Conglomerates

Microsoft - United States - Software & Services

Toyota Motor - Japan - Consumer Durables

Nestlé - Switzerland - Food, Drink & Tobacco

BHP Billiton - Australia/United Kingdom - Materials

Total - France - Oil & Gas Operations

Petrobras-Petróleo Brasil - Brazil - Oil & Gas Operations

Procter & Gamble – U. S. - Household & Personal Products

Wal-Mart Stores - United States - Retailing

Vodafone – U. K. - Telecommunications Services

Banco Santander - Spain - Banking

Johnson & Johnson – U. S. - Drugs & Biotechnology

ENI - Italy - Oil & Gas Operations

Company   Country   Industry
AT&T - United States - Telecommunications Services

IBM - United States - Software & Services

Orascom Construction Inds - Egypt - Construction

China Mobile - Hong Kong/China - Telecom Services

ICBC - China - Banking

Rosneft - Russia - Oil & Gas Operations

Intesa Sanpaolo - Italy - Banking

Telefónica - Spain - Telecommunications Services

Porsche - Germany - Consumer Durables

Lukoil - Russia - Oil & Gas Operations

Deutsche Bank - Germany - Diversified Financials

CCB-China Construction Bank - China - Banking

ArcelorMittal - Luxembourg - Materials

Vale - Brazil - Materials

GDF Suez - France - Utilities

UniCredit Group - Italy - Banking

Roche Holding - Switzerland - Drugs & Biotechnology

Company   Country   Industry
Novartis - Switzerland - Drugs & Biotechnology

Pfizer - United States - Drugs & Biotechnology

Siemens - Germany - Conglomerates

Hewlett-Packard – U.S. - Tech Hardware & Equipment

Samsung Electronics - South Korea - Semiconductors

Merck & Co - United States - Drugs & Biotechnology

Bank of China - China - Banking

Cisco Systems – U.S. - Technology Hardware & Equip

Sinopec-China Petroleum - China - Oil & Gas Operations

ENEL - Italy - Utilities

Unilever – Netherlands/U.K. - Food, Drink & Tobacco

BBVA-Banco Bilbao Vizcaya - Spain - Banking

Philip Morris International – U.S. - Food, Drink & Tobacco

Occidental Petroleum – U.S. - Oil & Gas Operations

GlaxoSmithKline – U.K. - Drugs & Biotechnology

Volkswagen Group - Germany - Consumer Durables

Verizon Communications – U.S. - Telecom Services

Company   Country   Industry
Barclays - United Kingdom - Banking

Mitsubishi UFJ Financial - Japan - Banking

Nippon Telegraph & Tel - Japan - Telecom Services

National Grid - United Kingdom - Utilities

StatoilHydro - Norway - Oil & Gas Operations

AstraZeneca - United Kingdom - Drugs & Biotechnology

Honda Motor - Japan - Consumer Durables

EnCana - Canada - Oil & Gas Operations

TNK-BP Holding - Russia - Oil & Gas Operations

Crédit Agricole - France - Banking

Saudi Basic Industries - Saudi Arabia - Chemicals

Coca-Cola - United States - Food, Drink & Tobacco

Oracle - United States - Software & Services

HSBC Holdings - United Kingdom - Banking

France Telecom - France - Telecommunications Services

Nokia - Finland - Technology Hardware & Equipment

MMC Norilsk Nickel - Russia - Materials

Company   Country   Industry

Fortis - Netherlands - Diversified Financials

Schlumberger - Netherlands - Oil & Gas Operations

Sanofi-Aventis - France - Drugs & Biotechnology

China Life Insurance - China - Insurance

Intel - United States - Semiconductors

Ecopetrol - Colombia - Oil & Gas Operations

Corning – U.S. - Technology Hardware & Equipment

Bristol-Myers Squibb – U.S. - Drugs & Biotechnology

PepsiCo - United States - Food, Drink & Tobacco

Berkshire Hathaway - United States - Diversified Financials

Oil & Natural Gas - India - Oil & Gas Operations

Abbott Laboratories – U.S. - Drugs & Biotechnology

Reliance Industries - India - Oil & Gas Operations

Apple – U.S. - Technology Hardware & Equipment

Nissan Motor - Japan - Consumer Durables

EDF Group - France - Utilities

United Technologies - United States - Conglomerates

Company   Country   Industry
Mitsubishi Corp - Japan - Trading Companies

Sumitomo Mitsui Financial - Japan - Banking

Commonwealth Bank - Australia - Banking

BG Group - United Kingdom - Oil & Gas Operations

Wyeth - United States - Drugs & Biotechnology

América Móvil - Mexico - Telecommunications Services

Sberbank - Russia - Banking

Loews - United States - Insurance

McDonald's - United States - Hotels, Restaurants & Leisure

Generali Group - Italy - Insurance

Google - United States - Software & Services

Tesco - United Kingdom - Food Markets

BNP Paribas - France - Banking

Largest Private Companies in the U.S. 2009

Company	State	Industry
Cargill	MN	Farm Products
HE Butt Grocery	TX	Grocery Stores

Company	State	Industry
Koch Industries	KS	Chemicals - Major Diversified
Fidelity Investments	MA	Asset Management
Chrysler	MI	Auto Manufacturers - Major
Cox Enterprises	GA	Entertainment - Diversified
GMAC Financial Services	MI	Financial Services
Flying J	UT	Oil & Gas Refining & Mrkting
PricewaterhouseCoopers	NY	Business Services
Toys "R" Us	NJ	Toy & Hobby Stores
Mars	VA	Confectioners
Meijer	MI	Grocery Stores
Bechtel	CA	Heavy Construction
Platinum Equity	CA	Conglomerates
HCA	TN	Hospitals
Aramark	PA	Business Services
Ernst & Young	NY	Business Services
Enterprise Rent-A-Car	MO	Rental & Leasing Services
Publix Super Markets	FL	Grocery Stores

Company	State	Industry
TransMontaigne	CO	Oil & Gas Pipelines
US Foodservice	IL	Food - Major Diversified
JM Family Enterprises	FL	Auto Manufacturers - Major

Appendix E: <u>Assets and Liabilities of Households:</u> <u>1990 to 2007</u>

[As of December 31 (14,613 represents $14,613,000,000,000). Includes nonprofit organizations.

Type of instrument	Total (bil. dol.)							% distribution		
	1990	2000	2003	2004	2005	2006	2007	1990	2000	2007
Total financial assets	14613	33285	34048	37096	39544	43218	45333	100	100	100
Deposits	3300	4350	5328	5706	6088	6733	7389	22.6	13.1	16.3
Foreign deposits	13	48	52	57	62	67	86	0.1	0.1	0.2
Checkable deposits and currency	411	279	329	294	156	122	78	2.8	0.8	0.2
Time and savings deposits	2485	3062	3986	4451	4921	5428	5880	17	9.2	13
Money market fund shares	391	960	960	904	949	1114	1344	2.7	2.9	3
Credit market instruments	1768	2556	2930	3213	3450	3667	3977	12.1	7.7	8.8
Open-market paper	94	97	106	136	164	188	160	0.6	0.3	0.4
Treasury securities	529	605	462	555	550	490	309	3.6	1.8	0.7

	1990	2000	2003	2004	2005	2006	2007	1990	2000	2007
Agency and GSE-backed securities 1	114	604	432	398	496	518	947	0.8	1.8	2.1
Municipal securities	648	531	704	743	821	866	916	4.4	1.6	2
Corporate and foreign bonds	245	618	1108	1255	1286	1469	1505	1.7	1.9	3.3
Mortgages	139	100	118	126	132	135	141	0.9	0.3	0.3
Corporate equities 2	1961	8199	5767	5938	5875	6178	5447	13.4	24.6	12
Mutual fund shares	512	2704	2904	3417	3840	4536	5082	3.5	8.1	11.2
Security credit	62	412	475	578	575	656	853	0.4	1.2	1.9
Life insurance reserves	392	819	1013	1060	1083	1164	1205	2.7	2.5	2.7
Pension fund reserves 3	3330	9188	9744	10655	11391	12324	12780	22.8	27.6	28.2
Equity in non-corporate business	3033	4677	5397	5986	6651	7330	7892	20.8	14.1	17.4
Miscellan-eous assets	254	379	489	542	591	631	709	1.7	1.1	1.6
Total liabilities	**3718**	**7398**	**9857**	**11035**	**12191**	**13454**	**14375**	**100**	**100**	**100**
Credit market instruments	3596	7009	9497	10575	11754	12948	13825	96.7	94.7	96.2
Home mortgages 4	2504	4818	6882	7838	8866	9854	10509	67.3	65.1	73.1

	1990	2000	2003	2004	2005	2006	2007	1990	2000	2007
Consumer credit	824	1741	2104	2219	2314	2418	2551	22.2	23.5	17.7
Municipal securities	86	138	178	189	205	227	250	2.3	1.9	1.7
Bank loans, n.e.c	18	65	53	35	48	96	131	0.5	0.9	0.9
Other loans	82	120	119	119	119	123	128	2.2	1.6	0.9
Commercial mortgages	83	127	160	175	201	230	257	2.2	1.7	1.8
Security credit	39	235	183	264	232	292	325	1	3.2	2.3
Trade payables	67	135	157	173	182	191	200	1.8	1.8	1.4
Unpaid life insurance 5	16	20	21	22	22	23	24	0.4	0.3	0.2

1) GSE = government-sponsored enterprises. 2) Only those
directly held and those in closed-end and exchange-traded
funds. Other equities are included in mutual funds and life
insurance and pension reserves. 3) See also Table 1177.
4) Includes loans made under home equity lines of credit
and home equity loans secured by junior liens. 5) Includes
deferred premiums.

Source: Board of Governors of the Federal Reserve System,
"Federal Reserve Statistical Release, Z.1, Flow of Funds
Accounts of the United States"; published 6 March 2008;
<http://www.federalreserve.gov/releases/z1/20080306

Appendix F: <u>More Great Quotes</u>

--Inspirational Quotes on Greatness--

Great spirits have always encountered
violent opposition from mediocre minds.

--- Albert Einstein

Each of us is great insofar as we perceive
and act on the infinite possibilities which lie
undiscovered and unrecognized about us.

--- James Harvey Robinson

Great things are not done by impulse,
but by a series of small things
brought together.

--- Vincent Van Gogh

Great things are done when men and
mountains meet.

--- William Blake

Great work is done by people who are not afraid to be great.

--- Fernando Flores

Great works are performed, not by strength, but by perseverance.

--- Samuel Johnson

Greater is he who acts from love than he who acts from fear.

--- Simeon Ben Eleazar

Greatness lies not in being strong, but in the right use of strength.

--- Henry Ward Beecher

--Famous Quotes About Success--

Victory becomes, to some degree, a state of mind. Knowing ourselves superior to the anxieties, troubles, and worries which obsess us, we are superior to them.

--- Basil King

We are told that talent creates its own
opportunities. But it sometimes seems that intense
desire creates not only its own opportunities,
but its own talents.

--- Eric Hoffer

We don't grow unless we take risks.
Any successful company is riddled
with failures.

--- James E. Burke

Victory is sweetest when you've known defeat.

--- Malcolm Forbes

We will often find compensation if we think
more of what life has given us and less
about what life has taken away.

--- William Barclay

Whatever you vividly imagine, ardently desire, sincerely believe, and enthusiastically act upon... must inevitably come to pass!

--- Paul J. Meyer

When ability exceeds ambition, or ambition exceeds ability, the likelihood of success is limited.

--- Ralph Half

--Quotes about Determination--

It's easier to go down a hill than up it but the view is much better at the top.

--- Henry Ward Beecher

It's the constant and determined effort that breaks down all resistance and sweeps away all obstacles.

--- Claude M. Bristol

Knowing is not enough, we must apply.
Willing is not enough, we must do.

--- Johann von Goethe

Leaders aren't born, they are made. And they are made just like anything else, through hard work. And that's the price we'll have to pay to achieve that goal, or any goal.

--- Vincent Lombardi

Let us not be content to wait and see what will happen, but give us the determination to make the right things happen.

--- Peter Marshall

--Other Motivational Quotes--

Men who are resolved to find a way for themselves will always find opportunities enough; and if they do not find them, they will make them.

--- Samuel Smiles

Mind is all that counts. You can be whatever you
make up your mind to be.

--- Robert Collier

More powerful than the will to win
is the courage to begin.

--- Unknown Author

Most of the important things in the world have
been accomplished by people who have kept on
trying when there seemed to be no hope at all.

--- Dale Carnegie

Life is either a daring adventure or nothing

--- Helen Keller

You've got to use what you've got,
to get what you want

--- James Brown

LIFE'S A BEACH, SO LIVE YOUR LIFE, 'CAUSE
THERE'S NO REASON, TO WONDER WHY, 'CAUSE
GOOD AND BAD TIMES, THEY COME AND GO,
SOMETIMES THE TIDE IS HIGH, SOMETIMES IT'S
LOW, LIFE'S A BEACH, SO LIVE YOUR LIFE, AND
LIVE EACH DAY, UNTIL YOU DIE, 'CAUSE FRIENDS
ARE THERE FOR YOU, THROUGH THICK AND
THIN, WHEN YOU'RE THE LAST IN LINE AND
WHEN YOU WIN

--- from the song: Life's a Beach,
by Luciano Illuminati

Yes, that's me when I'm singing, but this is no cheap ploy to
sell you to my other products. I believe in the power of my
own words to motivate people through songs as well. If I
didn't, would I be worthy of the authorship of this book?
Read the full lyric sheet on the next pages and go to my
website for more details on my music:
www.LucianoIlluminati.com

LIFE'S A BEACH

<u>CHORUS:</u> LIFE'S A BEACH, SO LIVE YOUR LIFE, 'CAUSE THERE'S NO REASON, TO WONDER WHY, 'CAUSE GOOD AND BAD TIMES, THEY COME AND GO, SOMETIMES THE TIDE IS HIGH, SOMETIMES IT'S LOW, LIFE'S A BEACH, SO LIVE YOUR LIFE, AND LIVE EACH DAY, UNTIL YOU DIE, 'CAUSE FRIENDS ARE THERE FOR YOU, THROUGH THICK AND THIN, WHEN YOU'RE THE LAST IN LINE AND WHEN YOU WIN

{verse 1}
I REMEMBER, BACK IN THE DAYS, WHEN I WAS YOUNG, MY FRIENDS AND I, PLAYED BASKETBALL AND HAD FUN, WE WOULD, STAY OUTSIDE ALL DAY 'TIL IT WAS NIGHT, 'CAUSE WHEN YOU'RE A KID IN THE SUMMER, EVERYTHING IS ALRIGHT, AND SOME KIDS LIKED SOFTBALL, SO THEY WOULD PLAY IT, FROM JUNE UNTIL THE FALL, AND WE WOULD PLAY ON THE SAND, DOWN AT THE BEACH, WHEN OUR FAMILIES TOOK US THERE, AT THE END OF THE WEEK, EVERYTHING WAS LOVELY, EVERYTHING WAS SWEET, NOT A CARE IN THE WORLD, THEN I START TO NOTICE GIRLS AND THEN I TRY TO GET THEM, TO NOTICE ME, BUT I'M STILL TOO YOUNG, TO DO LIKE THE TEENS.

CHORUS

{verse 2}

WHEN YOU'RE A TEENAGER, THINGS TEND TO
COMPLICATE, YOU THINK ABOUT GRADES
MORE AND THE FIRST PERSON YOU DATE,
WHAT DO GIRLS WANT, HOW DO YOU GIVE IT
TO THEM, HOW DO YOU FIT IN, WITH YOUR
CIRCLE OF FRIENDS, SHOULD YOU LISTEN TO
THEM, WHAT IS LOVE, WHAT'S THE MEANING
OF IT ALL, SHOULD YOU STARE AT THE PHONE
ALL DAY, SHOULD YOU CALL HER, WHY IS IT
HARDER, NOT TO BE LATE, ON A SCHOOL
NIGHT, WILL YOU GET ANY SLEEP TONIGHT,
YOU'VE GOT EXAMS TOMORROW AND MORE
QUESTIONS SEEM TO FOLLOW, PROM, COLLEGE,
THOUGHTS ABOUT YOU'RE FUTURE, 'CAUSE
YOU'RE NOT A KID ANYMORE, THAT'S FOR
SHORE, BUT YOU'RE STILL NOT GROWN
ENOUGH, TO LEAVE HOME.

CHORUS

SOLO

[verse 3]

I'M ALL GROWN UP NOW, STILL LIKE THE
PRETTY GIRLS MORE, STILL BUY MY COCONUT
JUICE, AT THE PHIL. IMPORTS STORE, DON'T
DELIVER PIZZAS FOR CHANELLO'S ANYMORE,
BUT I STILL LOVE TO CRUISE THE STREETS, OF
VIRGINIA BEACH AND MAYBE ONE DAY, I'LL
PLAY SOME GOLF, OR TAKE A BOAT OFF THE
DOCKS, AT RUDEE INLET AND LET THE LAZY
DAYS OF SUMMER ROLL, 'CAUSE I STILL LIKE IT
WHEN IT'S WARM, MORE THAN WHEN IT'S
COLD, 'CAUSE THE GIRLS LOOK HOT, ON
ATLANTIC AVENUE AND I WANT A CUTIE,
HANGING OUT AT THE BEACH TO, COME
WITH ME, TO THE VIRGINIA BEACH
AMPHITHEATER AND WE CAN HAVE A NIGHT
TO REMEMBER THAT...

CHORUS (x 4)

Carpe Diem!